Existential Battles
The Growth of Norman Mailer

LAURA ADAMS

Existential Battles
The Growth of
Norman Mailer

OHIO UNIVERSITY PRESS / Athens, Ohio

1888570

For Bob and Tom
and for Norman

ACKNOWLEDGMENTS

Grateful acknowledgment is made to the Liberal Arts Research Committee of Wright State University for their grants in aid of this work; to Molly Malone Cook and Scott Meredith, who facilitated its publication; and to Norman Mailer for his many generosities.

CONTENTS

Existential Battles
The Growth of Norman Mailer

INTRODUCTION:
THE THESIS AND THE CONTEXT

The Thesis

In 1959 Norman Mailer opened his literary manifesto, *Advertisements for Myself*, with the admission that he was "imprisoned with a perception which will settle for nothing less than making a revolution in the consciousness of our time."[1] The grand assumption in this statement lies not so much in Mailer's confidence in his own ability to create such a revolution as in the belief that a writer, especially a novelist, may wield enough power to force his society to change its direction. The belief that "it is the actions of men and not their sentiments which make history," a sentence which Mailer has called "the best . . . I ever wrote" (*Adv.*, p. 439), leads him to determine that a relationship of cause and effect should exist between writing and acting: "there is no communication unless action has resulted, be it immediately or in the unknown and indefinite future" (*Adv.*, p. 266).

What a writer's immediate or long-range effects may be are, of course, difficult if not impossible to determine, as Mailer knows. He believes, however, in a variation on Newton's Third Law, that if one's art and one's philosophy are important enough, their reverberations, no matter how ephemeral or long delayed, will be felt. It is through the written word, locked immutably in print, that Mailer believes

3

his influence will be most significant, although as we shall see he has by no means limited his potential influence to writing and has explored a variety of forms within that medium. The relative effectiveness of these various forms for Mailer's purposes will concern us later, but first the philosophy that moves and informs the art must be explained.

The first tenet of that philosophy is that life is better than death. On such a simple and indisputable basis, Mailer designs his life and his art in such a way as to sustain life and fight off death quite literally in some cases, more metaphorically in others. To Mailer there is no such thing as stasis, for at any given moment one is either dying or growing. In an interview in 1958 Mailer stated it this way:

> Ideally, what I would hope to do with my work is intensify a consciousness that the core of life cannot be cheated. Every moment of one's existence one is growing into more or retreating into less. . . . That the choice is not to live a little more or to not live a little more; it is to live a little more or to die a little more. And as one dies a little more, one enters a most dangerous moral condition for oneself because one starts making other people die a little more in order to stay alive oneself. I think this is exactly the murderous network in which we all live by now. (*Adv.*, pp. 355–56)

The need for growth in order to become and to overcome is the core of Mailer's metaphysics. Through this perspective, one can view Mailer's work as a process aimed at both creating new life and expanding existing life; for the alternative is contraction, a narrowing of horizons and of achievement, and, ultimately, the death of the spirit.

That process is concerned with altering the "consciousness of our time," by which Mailer means the complex network of attitudes which results in the behavior that moves our society in the direction it is taking, which he clearly sees as toward death. Each of his works, although they span more than a quarter century, contains the theme that the death of the human spirit is fast approaching, and that only a radical change from a death-producing, or "totalitarian," state to a life-producing one can arrest the progress of the disease which Mailer images as "cancer" or "the plague."

4

The Thesis and the Context

In essence, Mailer sees the machine technology and those who contribute to the furtherance of its power as the villains and the whole man as the victim. Leo Marx has shown us that the theme of the machine in the garden has been present in American literature since its inception, but in Mailer's version the machine has a human face, for finally the machine is man himself, product of a lengthy technological process, whose mind is divided into a complex of isolated compartments, whose senses have all but atrophied, and whose instincts are all but extinct, whose body functions at a remove from its mind, and whose spirit can scarcely be believed to exist. Through a revolution of his own making, in the manner of the God of Genesis, Mailer wishes to breathe life into this robot, to change it back into a man with all of his faculties reintegrated who is once more capable himself of producing life. While analogues to this "new man" may be found in the Renaissance, in frontier America, and in Romantic literature when human possibility seemed limitless, the Mailer hero will emerge from the crosscurrents of his times. The recreation of the human consciousness which Mailer envisions is to be accomplished through a series of small but meaningful victories over the death impulse. The basis for this view is Mailer's self-developed existentialism, considered by him and well documented to be American rather than European in nature and origin,[2] which can be summarized as follows: since death is the end of our lives both biologically and as the product of the process which moves our culture, the only way to live is to face the fact of that death and fight it off with all of one's resources. Extreme courage and honesty in the face of death or more often a destructive force outside of or within oneself are the weapons to be brought to each confrontation; and if one is victorious he extracts from his defeated opponent some of his force, which is then used to sustain and nurture his own life. The theory bears obvious affinities to Darwin's survival of the fittest, the more so because Mailer believes that the life of the species is at stake. His theory of violence, articulated most clearly in "The White Negro" and most powerfully and imaginatively in *An American Dream* (to be considered in subsequent chapters), is an extension of this concept and is largely responsible for Mailer's delayed admission to the American literary establishment. Ironically, it was not until he advocated the overthrow of a force which that establishment also found reprehensible—the president of the United States, the Pentagon, and "their" war in Vietnam—that Mailer won his tickets of admission in the forms of the Pulitzer Prize and the National Book Award in 1969 for *The Armies of the Night.* Ironically too, Mailer comes to believe through the experience he recorded in *The Armies of the Night* that unorganized violence such as that practiced by the demonstrators is self-defeating, and that one must use other means to defeat the enemy, means which capture real power.

On another level, to seek victory over what one considers evil and death producing is to strive toward the heroic condition. Mailer not only seeks it for himself but demands of those whom America has chosen as her heroes (John and Robert Kennedy, the Apollo astronauts) that they become authentic heroes, which is to say, that they close the gap between their images and their actions. The fact that Mailer himself has been engaged in a similar task, that is, of bringing in line the image ascribed to him as the author of the best seller *The Naked and the Dead* with a more authentic one, one which he had to grow into, is the subject of *Advertisements for Myself* and will be discussed at length in chapter one. In *Advertisements,* Mailer records the hard-won battles in which the strength of one's resources must be equivalent to a great victory even though only a minor one may result, because unless one overreaches the immediate goal he is not "growing into more" but "retreating into less."

Mailer, then, like many a hero in modern literature who must create the value of his own life, conceives of life as constructed on an existential plane from a series of moments, with growth taking the form of a line of movement which he has described as drawn by "going forward until you have to make a delicate decision either to continue in a different situation or to retreat and look for another way to go forward."[3] The line has breadth as well as length, for growth is

The Thesis and the Context

expansive: it pushes back the boundaries of consciousness and enlarges meaning and possibility. And "in widening the arena of the possible [for oneself], one widens it reciprocally for others as well" (*Adv.*, p. 327). In this sense the Mailer hero has more in common with the traditional hero than the contemporary antihero or nonheroic protagonist: he embodies what he believes the normative behavior of his society ought to be. So the vulnerable self is exposed to a spectrum of confrontations ranging from the most mundane to the most extremely dangerous, for the gains to be made from each are measurable. The most growth results from the greatest victory, but even a little growth is necessary to keep cancer from taking root and progressively destroying life.[4]

If growth is the theme of Mailer's work, it is also the method. "The method is married to the vision," he has put it.[5] There is nothing very startling in this pronouncement; what interests us here is that this theme and method have evolved into a consistent pattern which delineates both the nature and the form of the whole body of work. Believing that one's words and actions can excite others to act, Mailer makes his personality the "armature" of his work (*Adv.*, p. 203), not only in the sculptor's sense of a framework to flesh out artistically, but also in the biologist's sense of a protective covering serving an animal's offensive or defensive purposes.

It must be emphasized that the growth of Mailer the man does not have an entirely separate existence from that of Mailer the artist, because in the process of making himself (as well as his family and friends on occasion) a literary character, he has chosen public exploration and recording of his own most significant existential battles, mining them for his art. The use of himself as a character in his work, first seen in *Advertisements for Myself* and perfected by the time of *The Armies of the Night*, serves three functions.

First, the character "Mailer" is always at a stage of growth behind that of the narrator, enabling Mailer to study him with perhaps more detachment than he could bring to the creation of a fictional character who resembled himself in less tangible ways. Mailer has explained it this way: "the

7

writer . . . can deal with himself as a literary object, as the name of that man who goes through his pages, only by creating himself as a *literary* character, fully as much as any literary character in a work of undisputed fiction. . . . To the extent that he succeeds in making a viable character who will attract literary experience metaphorically equal to the ambiguous experience in his life which impelled him to write in the first place, so he will set out on the reconnaissance into the potentialities of an overpowering work."[6] In Wayne C. Booth's analysis of point of view, this distancing of the implied author from the narrator is crucial in enabling us to judge his actions.[7]

Second, through this literary character and his growing ability to create an alter ego and to distance himself from his work, Mailer unites its form and content in himself, bringing his art, his life, and the world as he sees it under his control; by developing a man big enough to encompass a given situation Mailer is developing an artistic ability to control not only a fictional but also the "real" world.

Third, the progress of Mailer's growth by expansion through confrontation and subsequent integration into the whole self, or thesis: antithesis: synthesis, therefore takes on for him enormous significance for the future of mankind. Mailer not only grows as an artist and into a representative hero, but his work itself, by enlarging the possibilities of art, may bring about the expanded human consciousness he is aiming at. In a true sense, Mailer's art is the creation of himself, because writing, or performing, as Richard Poirier has termed Mailer's artistic action,[8] is an existential act, a situation one enters involving a known risk and an unknown outcome in which he must rely upon his own wits. If the writing or the performance is good, he grows; if it is not, he pays. Further, the art is, in its ideal condition, existential for its audience as well, for the risk of engaging and being changed by Mailer's ideas is taken and the effects of the work are not immediately or finally known.

Obviously, such existential art presents problems in criticism. Certainly, the New Critical approach is insufficient for dealing with it, as is one which cannot take account of

The Thesis and the Context

Mailer's nonliterary performances and insists upon separating his disturbing public personality from his "art."[9] Richard Poirier goes part of the way towards a critical theory useful in interpreting Mailer when he notes that he "is best read as the author of a large work in progress,"[10] along with such writers as D. H. Lawrence, Henry Miller, and Thomas Wolfe. However, while conceptualizing about his writing as a performance consisting of a series of actions designed to create a unique shape out of recalcitrant matter and to turn a private conception into a public accomplishment,[11] Poirier does not seriously consider Mailer's performances which do not end up in print as part of that "large work in progress." "Only in writing," he states, "can Mailer exist in a form that embraces his contradictions; only in writing about a historical occasion after it is over can he give form to feelings that, expressed at the time, threaten to mutilate the form he is searching for in the occasion."[12] This conception of language as the artificial construct which a writer erects between utter chaos and what Mailer calls totalitarianism is one of Poirier's most significant contributions to an understanding of American literature generally and has been applied to Mailer, among other contemporary writers, by himself as well as by Tony Tanner.[13] Certainly Mailer's construct is more aesthetically pleasing in print than through any other method he has chosen; however, the philosophy he applies to his writing applies alike to his films and plays and his public appearances. I shall make more of this contention later. What the work of Poirier and others has established by now is that traditional approaches to Mailer are inadequate. An existential criticism is needed for purposes of evaluation even more than of interpretation of Mailer's work, and such a critical approach would have to accept Mailer's givens as its own and judge him by his own standards rather than insist that he conform to accepted literary tastes and practices. It would view his work as a process aimed at exploring the human subconscious and expanding its consciousness and would measure his success or failure in each undertaking by the extent to which he had done so as well as by the effectiveness of the form and his style. Above all, it would be

9

an adventurous criticism, one which broke new ground for the critic through his or her engagement with the work.

I have tried in this book to develop such a critical perspective on Mailer and have found that this means of entering a writer's world on his own terms in order to expose and connect his circuits breaks open one's own circuits as well as sets up a flow of current that can illuminate not only that world but one's own.

In terms of his own aims, I believe that the progress of Mailer's thought and his art can be traced through three books, each of which is the culmination and best expression of a phase of his development. Briefly, phase one consists of Mailer's emergence as an artist and his development of the coherent philosophy and artistic ambitions which found their first important expression in *Advertisements for Myself*. Phase two, culminating in *An American Dream*, is concerned with experimentation with forms of expression for his thought and enlarges the meaning of his existentialism. In phase three further experimentation leads to his finding an acceptable personal voice and the application of his vision to historical events in *The Armies of the Night*. Therefore, in subsequent chapters, each of these books will be examined in detail for what it reveals of Mailer's process of maturation, and the total statement of these chapters will be concerned with how Mailer moved from the style and themes of *The Naked and the Dead* to those of *The Armies of the Night*. The fourth phase is in progress. Having established himself as the spokesman-artist for events of national importance to Americans, Mailer's work of late has demonstrated not so much growth as the results of growth. He moves now toward the work of his life, a lengthy and ambitious novel he has promised himself and us for many years which in conception at least will be his masterpiece.

The Context

We shall be better equipped to assess Mailer's individual efforts as well as his total achievement by placing him, both initially and throughout this book, in the context most meaningful and useful for an understanding of his work, that of the mainstream of American literature.

A consideration of Mailer as an American writer may be approached either through the major figures whom he acknowledges as having influenced him or to whom he exhibits affinities, or through the aims and methods and attitudes which run through all of American literature. Both approaches may be drawn together by working backward from his contemporaries through the generation of writers which preceded him to the less tangible, more subtle connections which place him in the mainstream of American literature.

One notes that the literary title that Mailer most frequently assigns to himself is that of "the novelist." Although only five of Mailer's twenty-some books are novels, and although he has produced two plays, three films, and scores of stories and articles, not to mention his extensive nonliterary pursuits, it is significant that he emphasizes the role of novelist above the others. When he turns to literary criticism his "competitors" are always novelists, not poets, critics, playwrights, or film directors.[14] This is due not only to the fact that Mailer began as a novelist, but that for him novelwriting is the highest form of art. Even now he promises us the "big novel" he announced in *Advertisements for Myself*, presently underway, while publishing novelistic hybrids with historical, journalistic, autobiographical, and, recently in *Marilyn*, biographical components. He does not restrict himself to the novel because so much of his writing is of an occasional nature and because he wishes to experiment with vehicles of expression; but his preference for the novel and his emphasis on his role as novelist say something for the tradition in which he sees himself working, whose major writers are in the main novelists.

Perhaps Mailer views himself as capable of influencing his generation through his writing because he himself was profoundly influenced by the great generation of novelists who preceded him: Fitzgerald, Wolfe, Steinbeck, Dos Passos, Farrell, Faulkner, and especially Hemingway. But if the influence of the best work of these men fired Mailer's ambition to emulate them, the worst of their work inspired him to

11

outdo them. His yardstick for them as for all others, including himself, is whether their work was consistently worthy of their talents. In a key section of *Advertisements* entitled "Last Advertisement for Myself Before the Way Out," Mailer sets himself the task both of exceeding the limitations which in his opinion sapped the artistic energy of these men and of becoming mentor to the next generation of writers. While Cooper, Hawthorne, and James, among other of our novelists, have complained of the lack of native material for the American novelist, Mailer complains that America's talented writers burn themselves out in the heated struggle for success. I quote from the section at length, not only because it is the first important statement of the relationship I have mentioned between Mailer and his predecessors but also because of the metaphors of growth and destruction in which Mailer expresses the immensity of the committed writer's task.[15]

> If America is rich in talent, which it is, this wealth seems more than equaled by the speed with which we use up our talent . . . no one from that generation of major American writers who came before my own has put out work of the first importance since the war.
>
> Yet what a generation they were—how much more impressive than my own. If their works did not prepare us for the slack, the stupor, and the rootless wit of our years, they were still men who wrote strong, original novels, personal in style—so many of us were ready to become writers because of the world they opened.
>
> To call the roll today is depressing [the great but burned-out talents of Wolfe, Fitzgerald, Hemingway, Faulkner, Dos Passos, Farrell, and Steinbeck are considered]. One must go back to an earlier time, to Dreiser, to Lewis, and to Sherwood Anderson, in order to come across men who wrote across the larger length of their lives and had a career which came close to the limit of what they could do.
>
> America is a cruel soil for talent. . . . It stunts it, blights it, uproots it, or overheats it with cheap fertilizer [here Mailer castigates "publishers, editors, reviewers and general flunkeys" for promoting tastelessness and the reader for being their victim].
>
> So the strong talents of my generation, those few of us who have wide minds in a narrow undeveloped time, are left to wander through a landscape of occult herbs and voracious weeds, ambushed by the fallen wires of electrical but meaningless situations. . . . If it were not for some new generation coming to life—a generation which might be more interesting than my own, or so I must hope, it would be best to give up, because all desire is lost for talk-

The Thesis and the Context

ing to readers older than oneself. Defeated by war, prosperity, and conformity, the best of our elders are deadened into thinking machines, and the worst are broken scolds who parrot a plain house-wife's practical sense of the mediocre—worn-out middle-class bores of the psychoanalytical persuasion who worship the cheats of moderation, compromise, committee and indecision, or even worse, turn to respect the past. . . .

[Mailer concludes that his "new book"] will be fired to its fuse by the rumor that once I pointed to the farthest fence and said that within ten years I would try to hit the longest ball ever to go up into the accelerated hurricane air of our American letters. For if I have one ambition above all others, it is to write a novel which Dostoyevsky and Marx; Joyce and Freud; Stendhal, Tolstoy, Proust and Spengler; Faulkner, and even old moldering Hemingway might come to read, for it would carry what they had to tell another part of the way. (*Adv.*, pp. 436-39)

Several points should be emphasized here. First, Mailer locates the failure of the best talents of the 1930s in their having become psychological casualties of the war and of the postwar America which followed in its wake. Second, the job of the writer, he believes, is to consistently strive to widen the horizons of possibility to the limits of his talent for those who follow him, and he must have successors or he too has failed. Third, although Mailer's ambition to write was generated by the American novelists of his youth, his conception of the significance of writing was fostered by the example of the great nineteenth- and early twentieth-century minds whose writing can truly be claimed to have changed the shape of the future. Fourth, he envisions that a novel which he will write will have the power to produce such a change. Fifth, he wishes to claim his impending victory in the name of "our American letters," thus indicating the context in which he places himself. Finally, he does not here (and only to a limited extent does he later) see himself as a product of the novelistic traditions delineated variously by Richard Chase, R. W. B. Lewis, or Leslie Fiedler. He reaches back to the beginning of this century for his American models but as a rule not into the last.

In the articles entitled "Evaluations—Quick and Expensive Comments on the Talent in the Room" from *Advertisements for Myself* and "Some Children of the Goddess" from

13

Cannibals and Christians, Mailer proceeds through a list of his contemporaries—novelists all—whom he considers and generally dismisses as "competitors." Here are a few characteristic comments. On James Jones: "the only one of my contemporaries who I felt had more talent than myself," but who will not be worthy of it unless "he gives up the lust to measure his talent by the money he makes" (*Adv.*, pp. 426–27). On William Styron: "how much more potent he will seem to us, his contemporaries and his competitors, if he has had the moral courage to write a book equal to his hatred and therefore able to turn the consciousness of our time, an achievement which is the primary measure of a writer's size" (*Adv.*, p. 428). On William Burroughs's *Naked Lunch*: "the ideas have pushed into the frontier of an all-electronic universe . . . one gets intimations of a mind which might have come within distance of Joyce, except that a catastrophe has been visited on it, . . . a junkie's needle which left the crystalline brilliance crashed into bits" (*CC*, pp. 116–17). Following Burroughs's example, Mailer was himself to push into "the frontier of an all-electronic universe" in *Why Are We in Vietnam?*. On Saul Bellow's *Henderson the Rain King*: "the book is on the threshold of a stupendous climax—for the first time in years I had the feeling I was going to learn something large from a novel—and then like a slow leak the air goes out of the book in the last fifty pages. Dahfu is killed in a meaningless action, Henderson goes home to his wife, and the mystery that Bellow has begun to penetrate closes over his book, still intact" (*CC*, p. 127). Oddly, Mailer never mentions the parody of Hemingway written into the character of Henderson, which most other critics leapt upon.

Among those writers whom Mailer has admired more recently are Barth, Vonnegut, and Didion. I have heard him say too that *The Friends of Eddie Coyle* by George V. Higgins has some of the best dialogue he has ever read, and that he is intrigued by the fiction of Joyce Carol Oates, though he finds her a less gifted critic. The writers he admires tend to be visionaries like himself rather than crafts-

14

men. In large part Mailer's evaluations are based on one criterion: whether or not a writer has pushed back his own frontiers a little more with each work. One has to write a better book, perform in a different capacity from before—in some way outdo himself as an artist. In this sense "style is character," as Mailer has said, and in a key passage he reveals that his conception of writing is characteristic of that found in the American romance as defined by Richard Chase and others:[16]

> As he writes, the writer is reshaping his character. He is a better man and he is worse, once he has finished a book. Potentialities in him have been developed, other talents have been sacrificed. He has made choices on his route and the choices have shaped him.
>
> The writer, particularly the American writer, is not usually—if he is interesting—the quiet master of his craft; he is rather a being who ventured into the jungle of his unconscious to bring back a sense of order or a sense of chaos, he passes through ambushes in his sleep and, if he is ambitious, he must be ready to engage the congealed hostility of the world. If a writer is really good enough and bold enough he will, by the logic of society, write himself out onto the end of a limb which the world will saw off. He does not go necessarily to his death, but he must dare it. (*CC*, pp. 107–8)

Mailer is convinced that few of his contemporaries will take that dare; Hemingway's generation, on the other hand, produces ambiguous feelings in him. He finds it difficult to reconcile his early respect for these authors with his later bitter but uncompromising attitude toward their failures to live up to their talents. They chose—quite literally in the cases of Faulkner and Hemingway—death over life, and this is something Mailer cannot accept of one who could have been an authentic hero.

From Steinbeck, Wolfe, Dos Passos, and Farrell, the essential lesson Mailer learned was that when large minds engage great chunks of life, a strong personal style is the catalyst which turns data into art—a lesson exemplified in even his most recent work, though most directly as a derivative in *The Naked and the Dead*.

But Mailer's indebtedness to Hemingway is more complex. No other writer is more frequently mentioned by Mailer, nor in more mixed tones of contempt and awe. I will deal more specifically with the relationship in chapter one on *Advertisements for Myself*, a book designed in many ways to exorcise the still-living specter of Hemingway from Mailer's nightmares, although later comments reveal his incomplete assimilation into Mailer's image of himself. A few of the contours of that relationship, given below, can be seen in Mailer's work as recently as 1970. The epigraph to *Of a Fire on the Moon* is from Hemingway: "Now sleeps he with that old whore death. . . . Do thee take this old whore death for thy lawful wedded wife?"[14] The book begins:

> Hemingway's suicide left him wedded to horror. It is possible that in the eight years since, he never had a day which was completely free of thoughts of death [Mailer is annoyed at the time that the major newspapers did not elicit his response to Hemingway's death] the reactions of one of America's best-known young novelists would certainly be appropriate to the tragic finale of America's greatest living writer. . . . Hemingway had given the power to believe you could still shout down the corridor of the hospital, live next to the breath of the beast, accept your portion of dread each day. Now the greatest living romantic was dead. Dread was loose. The giant had not paid his dues, and something awful was in the air. Technology would fill the pause. Into the silences static would enter. It was conceivable that man was no longer ready to share the dread of the Lord. (*Fire*, pp. 3–4)

It can be seen, first, that Hemingway was Mailer's symbolic father: he was the authentic hero both as man and as artist whom Mailer wished to emulate. Second, Hemingway had achieved authority on the national level also, both among critics and general readers, and Mailer's own desire to be so acknowledged, to be accorded both popularity and significance in his lifetime, is necessary for his artistic goals. The Mailer who had been running for president "in the privacy of [his] mind" (*Adv.*, p. 15) since the popular and critical success of *The Naked and the Dead* proposed quite seriously though incredulously that Hemingway be the Democratic party's presidential candidate in 1956, mainly because he was "more man than most" (*Adv.*, p. 291). Mailer saw him as a mythic hero with the power to lead the forces of light against those of darkness and *to win*. Understood in these terms it is no wonder that Hemingway's suicide was devastating to Mailer. Third, Hemingway perpetrated two great failures for which Mailer could not forgive him: he deserted his followers and he killed himself. Of the first, Mailer says in *The Presidential Papers* that Hemingway "has been our greatest writer. It is certain he created my generation—he told us to be brave in a bad world and to be ready to die alone." In recent years, however, "we feel he has deserted us and produced no work good enough to justify the silence."[18] As Hemingway's disciple, Mailer invested him with Christlike powers, only to be forced to pronounce him a false Christ, a Judas in the end.

Concerning Hemingway's death, the following comment from *The Presidential Papers* should be interposed between the quotation given just above and that previously quoted from *Of a Fire on the Moon*: Mailer explores the possibility that Hemingway's death was not a suicide but a "reconnaissance from which he did not come back," a drastic attempt to arrest the progress of the plague through consecutively more dangerous incursions into death's territory until he entered too deeply to return (*PP*, p. 117). But although such an explanation would have redeemed Hemingway's manhood if not his sainthood for Mailer, it is clear from the opening page of *Of a Fire on the Moon* that he could not believe in it. Further, the enormity of the debt Mailer owed to Hemingway for providing him with a model on which to base his life and work amounted to an obsession, which in an interview in 1968 he described this way: "An obsession is created . . . in the wake of some event that has altered our life profoundly, or perhaps we have passed through some relationship with someone else that has altered our life drastically; . . . it's the most fundamental sort of event or relation. It has marked us, yet it's morally ambiguous."[19] This obsession with something in the past can cripple one's movement into the future, so one must come to terms with it either by breaking it or by entering it. The only way to make artistic use of it is to enter it, as Mailer has done in a continuing struggle to pay his dues so that he can grow free of Hemingway's shadow—and his curse.

Donald Kaufmann has dealt with the major similarities

and differences between Mailer and Hemingway, noting that the authors are alike in being legends in their own time, although their legends become notorious and over-shadow their writing. Both celebrate masculinity in sports such as boxing and bullfighting and in their life styles. Both, he notes, are "neoprimitives" with "a distrust of civilization and complication."[20] Apart from these points, the writers differ sharply: "More at home with the radical, the tabooed and the mysterious, Mailer veers from the Hemingway rapport with a 'clean, well-lighted' slice of experience," being a product of a more complex time than the earlier writer. Kaufmann also notes that Mailer is "a heavy-weight thinker," unlike his predecessor.[21]

Although their life styles are similar, their styles of writing are radically opposed. Mailer's has more in common with Faulkner's than with Hemingway's. Leo Braudy has characterized it as "a style that is unsure of the meaning it searches for, rather than a style, like that of the more realistic writers, that contains meaning and dispenses it in tight droplets."[22] In an "advertisement" for an early short story, Mailer notes the Faulknerian influence on his writing: "the prose is Salinger-ish, but the inspiration was from Faulkner. I had read The Sound and the Fury . . . and it had a long influence on me . . . Faulkner's style—which is to say, his vision—was to haunt my later themes like the ghost of some undiscovered mansion in my mind" (Adv., pp. 78–79). Faulkner's continuing subject, the curse Americans brought upon the virgin land, is also explored by Mailer in Why Are We in Vietnam?, a book which has been called a rewrite of "The Bear" and which echoes Faulkner's style as well as his theme.[23]

Richard Foster has noted the similarities between Mailer and Fitzgerald:

> . . . in the important ways Mailer's fiction is much more like Fitzgerald's than like Hemingway's. The kinds of men and women inhabiting their fictional worlds, and the archetypal relationships obtaining between them—the women as promissory images of value and possibility, the men as agents of motive and choice—are clearly similar.[24]

18

The Thesis and the Context

Besides sharing a "romantic moral sensibility,"[25] Foster goes on to say, it is a

> pattern of affirmative and idealistic impulses reflexively renewed or reborn in the face of disillusioning experience, plus the contemporaneous American subject matter which is the characteristic substance of their imaginative visions . . . [which] puts both [Fitzgerald and Mailer] in the main stream of American writers for whom the beauties and ambiguities of the "American dream" have been the inescapable motifs.[26]

Hemingway's life style, Faulkner's prose style, Fitzgerald's sensibility: Richard Poirier has summed up Mailer's stature with respect to these writers as well as those of Mailer's own generation in the following passage:

> *Why Are We in Vietnam?* and *The Armies of the Night*, along with parts of *Advertisements for Myself* and *An American Dream*, make Mailer easily the equal, it seems to me, of Fitzgerald and Hemingway, potentially of Faulkner. His accomplishment deserves comparison with theirs precisely because it is of a different kind and because it takes account of the varieties, evolutions, discontinuities, and accumulations of style since World War II. But he could not be to our time what they were to theirs without being in many important respects radically unlike them in the way he writes. No other American writer of this period has tried so resolutely and so successfully to account for the eclecticisms of contemporary life when it comes to ideas of form, of language, of culture, of political and social structures, and of the self.[27]

Mailer's relationship to earlier American writers should be seen first in light of what he considers in a typically dialectic way as "a war at the center of American letters." Using a Marxist metaphor, he sees the war as a class struggle between the "upper-middle class" which "looked for a development of its taste, a definition of its manners, a refinement of itself to prepare a shift to the aristocratic" and a lower-class literature "which grappled with a peculiarly American phenomenon—a tendency of American society to alter more rapidly than the ability of its artists to record that change" (*CC*, p. 95). The difficulty of the latter task was compounded by a concentration of power in the hands of those favoring the genteel literature and the necessity of the "lower class" novelist's divorcing himself from manners in order to describe "the social machine" (*CC*, p. 97), because he had not time to learn to describe both. Mailer sees Wolfe and especially Dreiser as the titan-heroes who undertook to bring light to the underlings. But they could not offer them the manners or tactics with which to enter the palaces of the gods themselves. This war of "Naturalism versus the Genteel Tradition" (*CC*, p. 98) had continued, according to Mailer, without producing a writer able to "clarify a nation's vision of itself" (ibid.) by uniting the two traditions, and in recent times the war has been transmogrified into "moral seriousness" versus camp, with Herzog and Candy as the "protagonists" (*CC*, p. 100). Mailer sees his own role as generating a literature which is essentially dead, not as carrying on a vital tradition. It will be seen later that he envisioned *An American Dream* as that book which would "clarify a nation's vision of itself" and win him acclaim as the American Tolstoy, and, I believe, he now asks the same of his large work in progress.

One of the most perceptive critics of our literature, D. H. Lawrence, with whom Mailer shares much of his vision (the romanticism, the necessity for the individual to connect with the "dark gods" within himself to achieve salvation, the clear demarcation of masculine and feminine principles, the use of sex as a metaphor for creation), identified the conflict at the heart of American life and the literature which has imaged it: that freedom and democracy are basically antithetical. America's attempts to work out a compromise between the two ideals have resulted in a tug-of-war between the proponents of each. The question of how much individual freedom one must sacrifice to the general welfare is as dynamic today as it was at the drawing up of the Constitution. As Lawrence sees it, "liberty in America has meant so far the breaking away from *all* dominion. The true liberty will only begin when Americans discover IT, and proceed possibly to fulfill IT. IT being the deepest *whole* self of man, the self in its wholeness, not idealistic halfness."[28] Lawrence saw further that a similar conflict is characteristic of American artists, a conflict between the intellect or conscious self and the subconscious or instinctual self.

20

The Thesis and the Context

In an essay entitled "Superman Comes to the Supermarket," intended to help elect John F. Kennedy to the presidency, Mailer sees a similar division in American life but links it to the aftermath of the First World War. Since then, Mailer believes,

> our history has moved on two rivers, one visible, the other underground; there has been the history of politics which is concrete, factual and unbelievably dull if not for the consequences of the actions of some of these men; and there is a sub-terranean river of untapped ferocious, lonely and romantic desires, that concentration of ecstasy and violence which is the dream life of the nation. (*PP*, p. 51)

Mailer saw the possibility of once again uniting these rivers in the person of Kennedy, whose charisma could inject a sense of adventure back into politics. He argued that

> it was a hero America needed, a hero central to his time, a man whose personality might suggest contradictions and mysteries which would reach into the alienated circuits of the underground, because only a hero can capture the secret imagination of a people, and so be good for the vitality of his nation; a hero embodies the fantasy and so allows each private mind the liberty to consider its fantasy and find a way to grow. . . . At bottom the concept of the hero is antagonistic to impersonal social progress, to the belief that social ills can be solved by social legislating, for it sees a country as all-but-trapped in its character until it has a hero who reveals the character of the country itself. (*PP*, pp. 55–56)

The hero whom a nation chooses is thus a metaphor for its ideal self, its dream image; and when America chooses an Eisenhower or a Lyndon Johnson for its president, it forces underground again the essential myth of the American Dream, that America was "the country in which the dynamic myth of the Renaissance—that every man was potentially extraordinary—knew its most passionate persistence" and "that each of us was born to be free, to wander, to have adventure and to grow on the waves of the violent, the perfumed, and the unexpected" (*PP*, pp. 52–53).

What Mailer has been attempting through his writing is to revive the myth of unlimited individual possibility for Americans, not in its bankrupt Horatio Alger version still presented in oral-formulaic political speeches, but in terms of uniting its instinctual life to its intellectual one, which is to say, to bring the myth to consciousness again where it had been before the closing of the Western frontier turned the myth inward. The deadly earnestness with which Mailer presents his thesis of heroism may be underscored by his belief that his essay helped elect Kennedy and the fearful responsibility he consequently felt, for he was not sure that Kennedy was the right man. If it turned out that there was more of the intellect than the romantic in him, the nation would continue to be schizophrenic. Mailer's search for a hero capable of embodying America's vision of itself and his failure to find him in the world of politics or fiction or even in the mythic "White Negro" who held his imagination for a time may be what led him to attempt to create a representative self as that American hero, who runs for president in his mind or for mayor of New York City in a campaign whose futility is measured by the distance we remain from Mailer's ideal.

Mailer's search for an ideal condition for the self has resulted in his being categorized by some critics as an American transcendentalist. But however much he may share with the transcendentalists, particularly Whitman's protean quality of creating a series of selves as a metaphor for the representative American and Emerson's ability to see the most in the least things, the essential passivity and naïve optimism of transcendentalism are foreign to his nature. While it is true that Mailer seeks transcendence through the synthesis of opposites within oneself and the nation as a whole, the world he views is a fallen one whose Adam, if he is to be heroic, must recreate mankind with more resistance to destructive forces. Mailer envisions the future in terms of an apocalypse, for he believes that there is a continuing war between God and the Devil for possession of the universe, and that God might lose. For Mailer, God

exists as a warring element in a divided universe, and we are a part of—perhaps the most important part—of His great expression, His enormous destiny; perhaps He is trying to impose upon the universe His conception of being against other conceptions of being very much opposed to His. Maybe we are in a sense the seed, the seed-carriers, the voyagers, the explorers, the embodiment of that embattled vision; maybe we are engaged in a heroic activity, and not a mean one. (*Adv.*, p. 351)

But he is never sure whether we are agents of good or evil. Unlike Melville for whom the meaning of such terms was relative (i.e., the tortoise is both dark and bright), Mailer could follow Mark Twain in imaging God and the Devil as identical twins. But Mailer can believe that one's intuitions can be trusted to tell them apart, saving him—so far—from the bitter pessimism of Mark Twain's later years.

Noting the characteristics of the American imagination as found in our best novelists, Richard Chase emphasizes that it "has been shaped by the contradictions and not by the unities and harmonies of our culture."[29] Residing in extremes of experience, unresolved ambiguities, and radical forms in a manner which Mailer would call schizophrenic, the American novel and the imagination which informs it are essentially romantic. Its central myth is that of Adam in the New World Garden and his expulsion after the Fall, the reenactment of man's encounter with an innocent land and the evil within himself; its characteristic theme that of the American Dream, its virtues, its flaws, and its effects on the American character.

The writers whom we place in the mainstream of American literature have all treated these themes, exhibited these tendencies, each bringing his angle of vision to bear on the American experience.

Michael Cowan is another critic who places Mailer in a line with writers from Emerson to Melville to Henry Adams to Faulkner in

the belief that American development is the product of a confrontation with virgin nature on a vast scale; the rapid and accelerating rate of social and psychological change that results from the American attempt to fill such large national space with a burgeoning machine technology; the heterogenous background of the Americans— immigrants all—partly melting into a new composite American, partly exacerbating social tensions as they whirl around the white Protestant center.[30]

Cowan is useful in tracing Mailer's affinities to Melville and

23

Henry Adams. Melville and Mailer share, he notes, immense literary ambition; obsessions with journeys into the terrifying mysteries of themselves; a "sense of adventure-ousness";[31] a proclivity for wild landscapes; and their quest for epic symbols, for example, Mailer's equivalent of Moby Dick, Apollo 11 as the leviathan hurling itself into space as mysterious as Melville's ocean; Mount Anaka in *The Naked and the Dead*; and, although Cowan doesn't mention it, the frozen Alaskan North in *Why Are We in Vietnam?*.

The Armies of the Night is a book which bears the closest resemblance to *The Education of Henry Adams*, but Cowan also notes general similarities between the two writers: "Like Adams, Mailer has increasingly treated his work as the rather ironic story of an education whose value as preparation for succeeding in or at least understanding a rapidly changing modern world is at best ambiguous. . . . Like Adams, Mailer sees history as an accelerating movement from unity to multiplicity."[32] Both writers, Cowan goes on to say, "proceed primarily by manipulating the ambiguities and shifting meaning of an immense series of dualities and by couching these dualities in sweeping and even melodramatic terms."[33] With this comment we are back to the divisions at the heart of the American imagination between good and evil, innocence and experience, the dream and the reality, the individual and the commonalty, which inhabit Mailer's imagination as well. While we have considered Mailer in conjunction with a number of our major writers, we might have chosen others as well—Emerson, Whitman, Hawthorne, Dreiser, Dos Passos, Farrell, or Steinbeck—for all mainstream American writers have had to grapple with this set of dualities.

I will suggest in succeeding chapters that Mailer has taken upon himself the task of making our most basic myth, the Adamic myth, exist on a literal level, in an effort to synthesize the thesis and antithesis present in much of our literature. He is engaged in developing "the deepest *whole* self of man" which Lawrence prophesied as the way to true liberty for Americans. Perhaps no other American writer has had a

The Thesis and the Context

vision of such magnitude. With what justification the following chapters will be concerned.

NOTES

1. Norman Mailer, *Advertisements for Myself,* p. 15. Further page references will be cited in the text, and the title will be abbreviated to *Adv.*
2. See especially Samuel Holland Hux, "American Myth and Existential Vision," pp. 179-211.
3. Paul Carroll, *"Playboy* Interview," p. 72.
4. Jayne Ellison, "Cancer, Personality Linked, Psychologist Says," p. 1. Until the results of research by Dr. Claus Vahnson were recently published, Mailer's theory on cancer had to remain metaphorical. Dr. Vahnson describes the "cancer personality" as "the man who is with the establishment, thinks discipline is good and expects high-level performance from others." He typically represses "anxiety, depression, hostility or guilt to a higher degree than all control groups."
5. Norman Mailer, *Cannibals and Christians,* p. 218. Further page references will be cited in the text, and the title will be abbreviated to *CC.*
6. Norman Mailer, "Up the Family Tree," p. 240 (reprinted in *Existential Errands*).
7. Wayne C. Booth, *The Rhetoric of Fiction,* pp. 149-65.
8. See Richard Poirier, *Norman Mailer* and *The Performing Self.*
9. For example, see Donald L. Kaufmann, *Norman Mailer,* p. xv.
10. Poirier, *Norman Mailer,* p. 58.
11. Poirier, *The Performing Self,* especially p. 88.
12. Poirier, *Norman Mailer,* p. 94.
13. See Poirier's *A World Elsewhere* and Tanner's *City of Words.*
14. With the notable exception of Robert Lowell in *The Armies of the Night,* whom Mailer places in a considerably larger context.
15. The number of quotations from *Advertisements for Myself* in this introduction requires explanation. Most of the ideas expressed in that book were rearticulated in later ones, but in *Advertisements* they received their first and, it may be argued, their most vital expression.
16. See especially Richard Chase, *The American Novel and Its Tradition,* pp. 1-13.
17. Norman Mailer, *Of a Fire on the Moon,* pp. 3-4. Further page references will be cited in the text, and the title will be shortened to *Fire.*
18. Norman Mailer, *The Presidential Papers,* p. 88. Further page references will be cited in the text, and the title will be abbreviated to *PP.*
19. Carroll, *"Playboy* Interview," p. 72.
20. Donald L. Kaufmann, "The Long Happy Life of Norman Mailer," pp. 347-59.
21. Ibid., p. 351.
22. Leo Braudy, "Norman Mailer: The Pride of Vulnerability," p. 15.

23. See Poirier's analysis of that style in *Norman Mailer*, pp. 147–48.
24. Richard Foster, "Mailer and the Fitzgerald Tradition," pp. 128–29.
25. Ibid., p. 135.
26. Ibid., p. 142.
27. Poirier, *Norman Mailer*, p. 121.
28. D. H. Lawrence, *Studies in Classic American Literature*, p. 7.
29. Chase, *The American Novel*, p. 1.
30. Michael Cowan, "The Americanness of Norman Mailer," p. 144 (reprinted in Laura Adams, ed., *Will the Real Norman Mailer Please Stand Up?*).
31. Ibid., p. 146.
32. Ibid., pp. 152–53.
33. Ibid., p. 153.

1

PHASE ONE: ADVERTISEMENTS FOR MYSELF

It may be said of *Advertisements for Myself* that the whole is greater than the sum of its parts. Critics of the "New" school would be inclined to agree with Marvin Mudrick's assessment that a large portion of the book is of interest only to thesis writers.[1] Those with a preference for novels view *Advertisements* as an important source book for explaining Mailer's later fiction, particularly *An American Dream*. Barry H. Leeds, for example, sees *Advertisements* as a stage toward later and more "valid" artistic forms, although he does not tell us how to determine such validity.[2] Others, mainly reviewers, have not found it necessary to recognize that the book contains anything besides "The White Negro" and Mailer's embittered comments on the sad state of life and literature in postwar America. In recent years, however, *Advertisements* has been recognized as a significant entity in itself, one whose form pioneered personal journalism, which has become a major genre in the 1960s and 1970s.

Earlier I described *Advertisements for Myself* as Mailer's "literary manifesto," for it is in this book that Mailer reveals his existential vision and declares his intention to become a major American writer. As a whole, then, *Advertisements* is not a mere collection of juvenilia and fugitive pieces interspersed with paranoic delusions of persecution and grandeur. It is Mailer's first major step toward the attainment of a heroic self; it is his not yet fully realized perception that the hero needed by America is not to be found between the pages of a novel; it is his declaration of independence from his literary forebears; above all it is the record of an artist's coming of age. If these are common enough American literary themes, the form in which they are presented in *Advertisements* is not. One critic has stated that the book has a movement but not a form.[3] I will argue that form in *Advertisements* is the pattern of that movement in terms of which Mailer has defined growth.[4] Mailer has frequently imaged the pattern of growth as a curve which is part of a circle, in turn part of a spiral.[5] The movement in these terms is circular and upward and symbolic of eternal life.[6] General Cummings in *The Naked and the Dead* sees only a segment of the spiral, "the curve of all human powers" which are limited by death (*ND*, p. 443).[7] By the end of *Advertisements*, in the prologue to the magnum opus Mailer then envisioned, the mysterious narrator has come to see all of time and growth in terms of the spiral. "The logic of his intuition" convinces him that "the natural spiral, wherever it appeared, was the mark of a complex of feeling . . . the form of his thought was also spiral: he would have to make that all but circular voyage through experience before he would come back to contemplate the spiral again" (*Adv.*, p. 476). The closed forms of the rectangle and triangle are seen as symbolic of the "narrow intense faith" of the Puritans, while the freedom and potentiality of the spiral are in opposition to such closed-mindedness (*Adv.*, p. 479). The cryptic exhortation at the end of *The Deer Park*, to "think of Sex as Time, and Time as the connection of new circuits,"[8] is clarified by the hypothesis in this prologue that "passive Time, Time on its way to death" may be denoted by parallel lines, while "Time as growth" connects the lines, showing them to be "once around the route in the expanding spiral of Being" (*DP*, p. 481). The spiral in movement is a gyre (the image may have been borrowed from Yeats), "God's gyre" in which each individual is a microcosm of God: "God is like Me, only more so" (ibid., p. 492). Ultimately the form of growth attains cosmic proportions for

Mailer when combined with the existential predicament of the individual's inability to know whether the gyre of his life is a part of God or the Devil.

The total form of *Advertisements for Myself* approximates that of a spiral. Mailer's "advertisements" serve as the connections between the parallel lines of the individual works he includes. The lines are horizontally parallel, like the rungs of a ladder, with the immature college piece, "A Calculus at Heaven," on the lowest rung and "Advertisement for Myself on the Way Out" on the top. What lies between is not, of course, so neatly progressive as this spiral metaphor suggests, but the chronological order that Mailer follows in the book is roughly equivalent to the progress of his growth as an artist. The concluding piece, while ending one book, very specifically points to future accomplishments and documents Mailer's conception of his work as a continuing process of growth.

Since a declared purpose of the book is "the intention to clear a ground for [the long] novel" (*Adv.*, p. vi) which he later abandoned, *Advertisements for Myself* may be seen also as an exorcism of the past, both that preexistential part of it which committed Mailer to the obligations of a successful first novelist and the frustrating years of searching for a philosophy of his own and a style appropriate to it. This meant closing the gap between what he wished to be and what he believed he was. It meant finding a direction and a method for growth and satisfying himself of his progress. By the time of *Advertisements*, he had progressed sufficiently to consider himself with some perspective and to have discovered a coherent vision of life to give artistic form. It is the further development of that vision for which I believe Mailer intended *Advertisements* to "clear a ground." His achievement in point of view in *Advertisements* is illustrative of his general development.

In *The Naked and the Dead* an omniscient undramatized narrator, to use Wayne C. Booth's terminology,[9] tells the story from the points of view of the various characters while maintaining an ironic tone which cues us that no final knowledge is possible. In Mailer's second novel, *Barbary Shore*, the impersonal narrator is dropped in favor of the first-person, dramatized, self-conscious narrator-agent, for Mailer has in the interim between the novels (1948 to 1951) developed the rudimentary existentialism that had appeared in *The Naked and the Dead* through the characters of Cummings, Hearn, and Croft. The point of view is thus in keeping with the limitations of the existentialist's knowledge to his personal experience. In order to know what goes on between McLeod and Hollingsworth in *Barbary Shore*, Lovett, the narrator, must actually be invited to their meetings, a situation explainable only by Mailer's conscientious preservation of the integrity of his chosen point of view. In *The Deer Park* an appeal to the willing suspension of disbelief is made by Sergius, a similar type of narrator, who claims imaginative access to vital scenes between characters and so renders them for us as if he had been there. Such gymnastics are solved with considerable wisdom in *Advertisements for Myself* by combining all the possibilities in the author himself. He is author, narrator, protagonist, reader, and critic. His work thus becomes self-contained. Later, in *The Armies of the Night*, he will separate more clearly these component relationships, for by referring to himself as "Mailer" he indicates that the narrator has progressed beyond the character and is more convincingly detached from the Mailer who has acted as opposed to the Mailer who is writing. The advantages of this technique will be examined later; it is not qualitatively different, however, from that of *Advertisements*. The point at which Mailer assumes these various roles is the point at which he is capable of doing so. In other words, he had to develop a vision of life, of his work, and of himself greater than any his first three novels had developed. The difficulties he experienced with his early narrators occurred because he as yet had no coherent vision of life and feared creating a character larger than himself. The fictional character he came closest to believing in was Sergius O'Shaugnessy whom he worked and reworked in and out of the novel and play versions of *The*

Deer Park, and who continued to make appearances in short stories and projected long novels. His long embattlement with the character of Sergius led him into those "rebellious imperatives of the self" (*DP*, p. 313) where he found the character most consistently demanding and rewarding to explore. The knowledge he gained of himself had future novelistic gains, for in *An American Dream* and *Why Are We in Vietnam?* he was able to create fictional first-person narrator-agents with inner lives of their own. Thus, the point of view in *Advertisements*, like the book itself, is a major breakthrough from past failures to future achievements.

For Mailer, the development of the self required radical freedom from the forces of totalitarianism, which he sees as all that separates us from our history, our instincts, the mysteries of our lives and our deaths. Totalitarianism is "a vast deadness, a huge monotony" (*PP*, p. 203), a mindless security which divorces us from guilt and responsibility for our actions. The striving to become equal to this freedom from self-limitation, to create a synthesis of the self with possibility, is the great strength of *Advertisements.*

Distrusting psychoanalysis, popularized in the 1950s, because it sets up a relationship akin to priest and confessor, allowing the confessor to transfer his insight and responsibility to himself to an agent of socialization-along-acceptable-lines, Mailer becomes a proselyte of self-analysis. He declares the aims of the novelist to be contrary to those of the psychoanalyst; the one is "a rebel concerned with Becoming," the other "a regulator concerned with Being" (*Adv.*, p. 282). *Advertisements for Myself* is a record of the self-analysis Mailer has undergone and which he seems to undergo before our eyes in the tone of his "advertisements," for the book is a kind of purgative, a therapy, a means of "clearing a ground" for greater work ahead. Richard Foster has discerned that *Advertisements* is written in the dramatic mode of elegy, "being shaped as a total action embodying patterns of divestment and purgation which yield up at last a clear prospect of fresh possibilities."[10] The metaphor of purgation is to become an important one in Mailer's future work, particularly in *Cannibals and Christians* and *Why Are We in Vietnam?* where it is given national significance. Here we see Mailer characteristically testing his ideas before applying them further.

Aside from the advertisements, the matter of the book is chronologically presented and consequently reveals the progression of Mailer's struggle with himself and the tentative self-confidence won by the book's end. From the outset, at least a dual tone is operating in the book. On the one hand, through the act of advertising himself, Mailer courts an audience because it is indispensable to his stated revolutionary purpose; on the other, he ridicules that audience for not being equal to the task of comprehending him. On another level, Mailer struggles for his own integrity, the public be damned. The first sentence of the book proper illustrates all three of these attitudes: "Like many another vain, empty, and bullying body of our time, I have been running for President these last ten years in the privacy of my mind, and it occurs to me that I am less close now than when I began" (*Adv.*, p. 15). It is to the presidency of American letters if not of the United States that Mailer aspires, and one must be elected president. At the same time he identifies himself with the typical candidate's "vain, empty, and bullying" nature, which observation is not calculated to endear him to the voters. On the third level, the flat honesty of the last clause redeems the sentence and the sentiment. The conflicting tones of solicitation, arrogance, and humility are characteristic of the advertisements which bind the book together because the justifications for Mailer's self-confidence were yet to be demonstrated to the voters, a situation of which Mailer is fully conscious. That "I am still at this formal middle of my life a creator of sentiments larger than my work" Mailer recognizes even at the end of *Advertisements* (p. 439). However, he believes that his "present and future work" will have "the deepest influence of any work being done by an American *novelist* in these years" (*Adv.*, p. 15, the italics are mine). *Advertisements* is an important step toward closing the gap between ambition and goal, and the gap can be closed only by the difficult inward search for the style which bears the deepest relation to the self. The magnitude of that difficulty is expressed in the book's third paragraph:

> There was a time when Pirandello could tease a comedy of pain out of six characters in search of an author, but that is only a whiff of purgatory next to the yaws of conscience a writer learns to feel when he sets his mirrors face to face and begins to jiggle his Self for a style which will have some relation to him. I would suspect it is not possible, no more than one can remake oneself signature for signature, but I have to admit I am not suited for this sort of confrontation despite two novels put down in the first person and a bloody season of overexpressed personal opinions as a newspaper columnist. To write about myself is to send my style through a circus of variations and postures, a fireworks of virtuosity designed to achieve . . . I do not even know what. Leave it that I become an actor, a quick-change artist, as if I believed I can trap the Prince of Truth in the act of switching a style. (*Adv.*, pp. 15-16)

Despite the elusiveness of the "Prince of Truth" Mailer does indeed set out to trap him. One learns about himself only by purposely exposing his vulnerable self to confrontations whose outcome is unknown and therefore dangerous to the self, an existential situation by Mailer's definition, and any self-dramatization realized as a consequence must either be accepted as a true enactment of a portion of one's nature or rejected as a false one. Such enactment of previously undeveloped aspects of the self has had the greatest importance in the progress of Mailer's life and work, causing great dismay to readers and critics who, just when they think they have categorized Mailer, are bewildered by his unpredictable shifting of roles. Many of these self-enactments have been sensational, ranging from the stabbing of his second wife to publicly denouncing the president of the United States in "obscene" language to running for mayor of New York. Certain actions carried out in private have become public by their nature, as is the case with the stabbing incident; while most which have won Mailer notoriety are undertaken in public, because he views them as legitimate functions of the artist as Public Voice, a role Mailer has laid claim to with increasing legitimacy in recent years.

Also, one may view this trying on of different hats, as the trying on of different forms of writing, as directed at exploring the limits of the self.

Advertisements for Myself is the recognition that such an exploration was necessary. The premise on which *Advertisements* is based is that Mailer has experienced defeat as a writer, which he blames alternately on a totalitarian society that stifles growth and on himself for not having the strength and courage to mature in spite of that society. The writers and thinkers of the thirties had formed his early political and literary concepts and, as with any youthful ideas, Mailer had to alter them on the basis of later experience. Those who note the derivative nature of *The Naked and the Dead* both philosophically and formally[11] tend to ignore the fact that Mailer experienced combat in the Pacific theater. He admits that his first thoughts after Pearl Harbor were concerned with "whether it would be more likely that a great war novel would be written about Europe or the Pacific" (*Adv.*, p. 24), so his aspirations to write such a novel were formed prior to his experience of war and must have colored his impressions of it. But although the extreme pessimism and dehumanization of the soldiers in *The Naked and the Dead* may be accounted for in part by the inherited philosophical bias of the depression era, it is also attributable to his personal experience as a soldier. The fascination with power which he exhibits in the characters of General Cummings and Sergeant Croft, for example, is very much his own. Mailer tells us that he "had formed the desire to be a major writer" before he was seventeen, in his first semester at Harvard (*Adv.*, p. 23). By Mailer's lights, being a major writer also meant wielding power, being in a position to "mold the curve" of human life as Cummings wished to do. Others have noted that Mailer is both attracted and repelled by the notion of a concentration of power in the hands of one individual.[12] Repelled by his belief that we cannot know if we use power for good or ill in the overall cosmic battle or indeed if we are being used by it, Mailer also feared his own newfound existential freedom. He records that the experiences of the years following the catapulting success of *The Naked and the Dead* justified that fear, and I quote at length from this key passage:

> . . . if once I had been a young man whom many did not notice, and so was able to take a delayed revenge—in my writing I could analyze the ones who neglected to look at me—now I came to know that I could bestow the cold tension of self-hatred, or the warmth of liking oneself again, to whichever friends, acquaintances, and strangers were weak, ambitious, vulnerable and in love with themselves.
>
> This was experience unlike the experience I had learned from books, and from the war. . . . It took me years to realize that it was my experience, the only one I would have to remember, that my apparently unconnected rat-scufflings and ego-gobblings could be fitted finally into a drastic vision, an introduction of the brave to the horrible, a dream, a nightmare which would belong to others and yet be my own. Willy-nilly I had had existentialism forced upon me, I was free, or at least whatever was still ready to change in my character escaped from the social obligations which suffocate others. I could seek to become what I chose to be, and if I failed—there was the ice pick of fear! I would have nothing to excuse failure. I would fail because I had not been brave enough to succeed. So I was too much free. Success had been a lobotomy to my past, there seemed no power from the past which could help me in the present, and I had no choice but to force myself to step into the war of the enormous present, to accept the private heat and fatigue of setting out by myself to cut a track through a new wild. (*Adv.*, p. 86)

It was at this early turning point in his career that Mailer began to have very much more at stake as a writer than he had had in *The Naked and the Dead*. This is why the subsequent popular and critical failures of his next two novels, *Barbary Shore* and *The Deer Park*, were so devastating. Hence the defensive tone of *Advertisements* and its issuance as a manifesto. If the success of *The Naked and the Dead* cut him off from his Brooklyn-Jewish past, the failures of *Barbary Shore* and *The Deer Park* cut him off from his dreams of power. From this point on he became distrustful of public opinion of his work and worked at becoming his own critic, the one he could be sure would follow the injunction he issued as an epigraph to *The Deer Park*: "Please do not understand me too quickly."

Although Mailer arrived at these positions independently, he was aware of their similarities to the career of Ernest

Hemingway and was most careful to emphasize the differences. Hemingway, he maintained, had secured his reputation on the knowledge that "he would have to campaign for himself, that the best tactic to hide the lockjaw of his shrinking genius was to become the personality of our time." Although Hemingway "did a lot of things which very few of us could do," Mailer goes on, "for all his size, and all we've learned from him about the real importance of physical courage, he has still pretended to be ignorant of the notion that it is not enough to feel like a man, one must try to think like a man as well." The essential lesson Mailer has learned from him, however, is that

> he's known the value of his own work, and he fought to make his personality enrich his books. . . . An author's personality can help or hurt the attention readers give to his books, and it is sometimes fatal to one's talents not to have a public with a clear public recognition of one's size. The way to save your work and reach more readers is to advertise yourself, steal your own favorite page out of Hemingway's unwritten Notes From Papa On How The Working Novelist Can Get Ahead. (*Adv.*, pp. 18-19)

While accepting Hemingway's methods of relating the public and private selves, Mailer declares his independence from Hemingway's distrust of abstract thoughts. Aware of the limited accomplishments of his generation, he sees that nevertheless

> we are the cowards who must defend courage, sex, consciousness, the beauty of the body, the search for love, and the capture of what may be, after all, an heroic destiny . . . it has been our act of faith, our attempt to see—to see and to see hard, to smell, even to touch, yes to capture that nerve of Being which may include all of us, that Reality whose existence may depend on the honest life of our work, the honor of ourselves which permits us to say no better than we have seen. (*Adv.*, pp. 21-22)

So ends the "First Advertisement for Myself," which along with all other such advertisements in the book make up what Mailer refers to in his "Second Table of Contents" as the "Biography of a Style."

In part one, "Beginnings," the first selection is a forty-page story written in 1942 while Mailer was at Harvard entitled

"A Calculus at Heaven." While Mailer does not recommend the story "except for those who have curiosity about my early work," he concedes that it makes "an interesting contrast to *The Naked and the Dead,* for it is an attempt of the imagination (aided and warped by books, movies, war correspondents, and the liberal mentality) to guess what war might really be like" (p. 24). It is a less interesting contrast to *The Red Badge of Courage,* also an imaginative response to war, and Mailer's modesty concerning it is very much in order. One might notice the use of several techniques which appeared later in *The Naked and the Dead.* The story has no particular plot, rather consisting of men placed in a situation and reacting to it. Storytelling has never been one of Mailer's fortes, but he had consistently used such a situational device; indeed, it is the basis of his existential philosophy. Mailer focuses on a number of individuals from different ranks, as in *The Naked and the Dead,* with flashbacks equivalent to the "Time Machine" sections of the novel. Although these sections have been frequently cast as derivations solely from the portraits and "Camera Eye" sections of *U.S.A.,* I think that Faulkner's influence is discernible in these distortions of time, for Mailer had read *The Sound and the Fury* a year earlier and claimed, as we know, to have long been influenced by it (*Adv.,* p. 78). Indeed, temporal distortions were to have increasing significance in Mailer's developing vision. "Destroy time, and chaos may be ordered" is the stated concept in a later story (*Adv.,* p. 173).

The character of the Captain in "A Calculus at Heaven" is that of an antiintellectual, agnostic artist figure, improbably named Bowen Hilliard, who can be claimed as a descendent of Hemingway and a romanticized version of Mailer himself, as well as the prototype for Lieutenant Hearn in *The Naked and the Dead.* Hilliard expresses the story's theme:

> "in America, men live, work and die without even the rudest conception of a dignity. At their death . . . well then they wonder what the odds are on a heaven, and perhaps they make futile desperate bets on it, adding up their crude moral calculus, so that if the big team,

heaven, comes through, and wins, and therefore exists, they will be
able to collect their bets that evening." (*Adv.*, p. 38)

Fortunately, Mailer becomes much more adept at handling a metaphor, although the extended metaphor is characteristic. This story also illustrates the type of point of
view Mailer used in his first novel, that of an undramatized
narrator focusing attention on one or more third-person centers of consciousness. More important here is Hilliard's
agnosticism: on the one hand, his desire to believe that life
has meaning and, on the other, his having to face the fact of
his own death in war. Hilliard is the modern alienated man
who hasn't quite found something to believe in, hasn't quite
become an existentialist, much like Hearn in *The Naked
and the Dead*, whose youthful idealism turns to an almost
naturalistic cynicism in war. Certainly Hearn's death is
naturalistic: it comes in an unguarded moment when he unknowingly exposes himself to enemy gunfire during what
should have been a small victory for him, leading his pla-
toon on a dangerous patrol. Similarly, the amoral Sergeant
Croft, prototype of Marion Faye and the White Negro, is pre-
vented from achieving his goal, the conquering of Mount
Anaka, Mailer's White Whale of a mountain, by a chance
encounter with a hornet's nest. The fatalism of the enlisted
men, buffeted by forces over which they have no control, is
contrasted most sharply by General Cummings's belief that
"Man's deepest urge is omnipotence" (*ND*, p. 255), to become God. Cummings, however, is undercut by authorial
point of view to the status of a megalomaniac.

While seeds of Mailer's existentialism are planted in this
novel, the persuasive tone is naturalistic, which is rein-
forced by the use of an omniscient narrator. Mailer's move
from this uneasy naturalism to existentialism lies in his
coming to believe that an individual must assume responsibility for his own destiny, and that God depends on the outcome of human action.

Mailer does not include excerpts from *The Naked and the
Dead* in *Advertisements for Myself* for two probable reasons: one, the novel was a best seller and presumably

needed no advertisement (a presumption characteristic of Mailer with respect to his work and his public image, largely because of the attention he has received from the mass media); and two, the work since *The Naked and the Dead* was of a different kind—less naturalistic and derivative, more romantic and original both philosophically and stylistically. *The Naked and the Dead* is an excellent novel; many critics consider it the best novel to come out of World War II, and certain traditionalists still think it the best of Mailer's work. There are many good accounts of the novel,[13] however, and I will not discuss it in detail here because it was written before the birth of Mailer's existentialism, which, indeed, arose partly out of the dislocation he experienced between the success of *The Naked and the Dead* and the failure of the novels which followed. *Advertisements* is the culmination of the phase of Mailer's work begun after the war novel.

Another early achievement in part one, a story called "The Greatest Thing in the World," which won first prize in a contest in 1941, is notable for revealing how early the idea that what was earned dangerously was worthwhile appeared in Mailer's work. A Hemingway influence is indicated, and with modifications the concept occupies a central position in Mailer's later existentialism.

Part two of *Advertisements for Myself*, "Middles," quite appropriately begins with excerpts from *Barbary Shore*. The "prominent and empty" Mailer of the years between the two novels (1948 to 1951), who "had to begin life again" (*Adv.*, p. 85), began it through Mikey Lovett, whose amnesia is akin to Mailer's own "lobotomy" of his past. The book's flounderings are apparent to Mailer for he claims it was "a book to emerge from the bombarded cellars of my unconscious, an agonized eye of a novel which tried to find some amalgam of my new experience and the larger horror of that world which might be preparing to destroy itself" (*Adv.*, p. 87). Yet he postulates that

> if my work is alive one hundred years from now, *Barbary Shore* will be considered the richest of my first three novels for it has in its high

fevers a kind of insane insight into the psychic mysteries of Stalinists, secret policemen, narcissists, children, Lesbians, hysterics, revolutionaries—it has an air which for me is the air of our time, authority and nihilism stalking one another in the orgiastic hollow of the century. (Ibid.)

He recently inscribed a first edition of *Barbary Shore* to me as "this first book on conspiracy." Mailer is one of the book's few critics not to treat it as a realistic novel and consequently to give it failing marks. The "psychic mysteries" have been the subject of much of his work and are a continuing source of fascination to him. That *Barbary Shore* is a well-made novel not even Mailer would argue; that it contains something of value is not too strong a claim to make for it. John Stark has argued that the novel is the basis for Mailer's best work because his "Manichean vision . . . reaches its mature complexity" therein.[14]

The allegorical nature of the book and its characters is often noted. Perhaps a student of Freud could make a case for its having the structure of a nightmare. Certainly there is a real structural conflict between the initiation story of Mikey Lovett and that of the fascistic nature of socialism under Stalin presented in the form of a tedious dialogue between McLeod and Hollingsworth. Once the author is released from the obligation to be "realistic," however, the book can bear almost as much weight as a medieval dream vision which ends where it began (with the repetition of the opening sentence in the case of *Barbary Shore*, borrowed from Melville) and in the meantime is not obliged to maintain a consistent literal level.[15] The narrator-hero of a dream vision generally wanders until his instruction in virtue is taken over by a guide. From this point on he reports what he has seen or heard and is not usually an active participant, although he is obliged to become one upon awakening from a dream. Lovett's role is similar, and in the book's context suggests Arthurian parallels, some of which Leeds has noted.[16] The relationships with Guinevere and Lannie (a perverted Launcelot) are wanderings; those with McLeod and Hollingsworth are instruction, and Lovett becomes the agent of what good can be taken from the book: the "remnants of [McLeod's] socialist culture"[17] to be protected in troubled times until it can be restored to its rightful place of power. McLeod is Lovett's guide and a spiritual King Arthur, passing his heritage on to Sir Bedivere whose death does not exclude the future attainment of Avalon, but whose immediate result is Barbary.

Without overstating the parallels, I must suggest those of the book to another badly received American novel by a popular author which it resembles in flaws as well as virtues: *The Blithedale Romance.*[18] The socialist-turned-fascist zeal of the Hollingsworth in each book is an obvious parallel. The roles of Miles Coverdale and Mikey Lovett are likewise similar, that is, to be accessible to the action in order to report it and to become the custodians of its moral import. Their initial amorality gives way through initiation to a certain amount of wisdom, particularly of the failings of socialist endeavors due to human limitations. What both books lose in plausibility they gain in mood and atmosphere, like true American romances. A further parallel to Hawthorne is seen in the ending of *Barbary Shore*, this time compared with *The Scarlet Letter.* Leeds has noted the similarities of Pearl and Monina.[19] In addition, at the end of *Barbary Shore*, McLeod, having earlier acknowledged that he is Monina's father, dies, and the child, now capable of human emotion, cries for him. She is then given into the hands of her mother's adulterous, evil lover, Hollingsworth. The situation might have provided a nightmare ending to *The Scarlet Letter.* One might also note in this context the similarity of the names Hollingsworth and Chillingworth.

I have been suggesting that *Barbary Shore* has considerably more imaginative power than Mailer's earlier work and an integrity of its own, which is evident when it is compared to works with which it shares concerns instead of to "realistic" novels, as has too often been the case. It illustrates Mailer's artistic growth acquired by his delving into the materials of the subconscious hitherto unexplored by him. In addition, the novel shows a progression in theme from a realization of the bankruptcy of Stalinism to the conclusion that while socialism may provide hope for an indefinable future, what is needed at present are individuals courageous enough to withstand the encroachment of totalitarianism. Mailer's purpose in including ten pages of excerpts from the novel in *Advertisements for Myself*, delineating his characters and their relationships with each other, must have been to encourage a full reading of it and a more sympathetic one than previously possible, appearing as it did at the beginning of the Korean War and the McCarthy era which in its own way it prophesied. Mailer marks the novel as "a first step toward work I will probably be doing from now on . . . an entrance into the mysteries of murder, suicide, incest, orgy, orgasm, and Time" (*Adv.*, p. 99) and notes that "much of my later writing cannot be understood without a glimpse of the odd shadow and theme-maddened light *Barbary Shore* casts before it" (p. 87).

The second major step was taken in *The Deer Park*, but prior to that Mailer spent a great deal of time foundering. The short stories he includes in *Advertisements* from the period between *Barbary Shore* and *The Deer Park* (1951 through 55) are in his opinion regressive since he "was not trying for more than [he] could do" (*Adv.*, p. 100). A slim piece called "The Notebook" explores the Hawthornesque theme of the writer as observer rather than participant and is indicative of Mailer's ability to separate the roles, though not yet to combine them in himself.

The next major piece in *Advertisements for Myself* is "The Man Who Studied Yoga," intended as a prologue to an eight-volume novel, a kind of *Piers Plowman* or *Finnegan's Wake*, conceived as eight stages of the dream of "a minor artist manqué" about "the adventures of a mythical hero, Sergius O'Shaugnessy, who would travel through many worlds, through pleasure, business, communism, church, working class, crime, homosexuality, and mysticism" (*Adv.*, p. 143). The element of time was to be distorted, as in a dream. The contemplated novel proved to be overwhelming and was abandoned by the end of the first draft of *The*

Deer Park. From the experience of struggling with the huge novel, Mailer began to develop a style both more imaginative and more disciplined than those of *The Naked and the Dead* and *Barbary Shore.* "The Man Who Studied Yoga" experiments with a first-person omniscient narrator who has the power to imagine himself as different characters and survey them with some detachment. Such a point of view is a progression beyond that of the third-person undramatized narrator of *The Naked and the Dead* and the first-person self-conscious narrator-agent of *Barbary Shore;* in fact it is a combination of the advantages of each; it is a way of knowing what one could not plausibly know while maintaining distance from the character since he exists only in the imagination, and it is in fact a dramatized version of the self as failure. By depicting a "minor artist manque" who "has wanted to be a serious novelist and now merely indulges the ambition" and who shies away from new experience (*Adv.*, p. 146), Mailer creates an alter ego, separating himself from the fears and failures he acknowledges in *Advertisements.* This is an example of the self-analysis Mailer engages in throughout the book when he plays a role he creates and then evaluates his performance.

In the story, Sam and his wife Eleanor are satirized as patients of the psychoanalyst Dr. Sergius (a version of O'Shaugnessy), who substitute the jargon of psychoanalysis, which conveniently names and supplies causes for all human failings, for the difficult introspection which would yield real knowledge of the self. Sam is frustrated by the disparity between his dreams of affecting history (he quotes as his own Mailer's maxim that "it is the actions of men and not their sentiments which make history" [*Adv.*, p. 152]) and his rejection of the world he meets in the pages of his newspaper. His conflict is illustrated by the central situation of the story. A group of the Slovodas' friends, all engaged in humanitarian occupations (lawyer, teacher, welfare worker), gather to watch a pornographic movie. The movie, entitled "The Evil Act," arouses the group, but instead of admitting this they feel obligated to dominate the film intellectually by discussing it as art. The schizophrenic and hypocritical nature of American life which is to be Mailer's constant theme finds metaphorical expression here in a more mature fashion than it had in any of Mailer's previous work.

The story, as the intended prologue to the eight-volume novel, gains richness from its metaphorical pattern. Seeds of all of that novel's themes are planted here as is the nebulous character variously depicted as Dr. Sergius, Cassius O'Shaugnessy, and Jerry O'Shaugnessy, who has been everywhere and done everything, the romantic hero who is Sam's alter ego and antiself and by implication Mailer's desired self. The Sergius O'Shaugnessy variations are metaphoric equivalents of the styles of living which Sam and his group are afraid to assume and are illustrative of the kind of viable literary character Mailer meant to "attract literary experience metaphorically equal to the ambiguous experience in [the writer's] life which impelled him to write in the first place" (cf. Introduction, p. 8). In other words, the writer seeks to embody his experiences, ambiguous as to their essential goodness or evil, in characters who express that ambiguity. He is then in control of the ambiguity and may explore his implications in a way he could not in his own life. What Mailer does up until the writing of *Advertisements for Myself* is to create separate fictional characters who approximate aspects of himself which he has been able, through his self-analysis, to identify and give form to. When Mailer becomes aware of this process enough to articulate it, he is able to deal with himself more objectively. He comes to identify the act of imagining with the probing of the subconscious self through writing. In an article written in 1967 Mailer articulates this concept more clearly.[20] He thinks that each of us carries around in his subconscious mind the stuff of a "huge and great social novel" consisting of our raw experiences. Something he calls "the navigator," a faculty which functions similarly to the ego on the id, charts its way through the massive data of our past experience and brings it to bear on the present. The navigator, like

44

the author of a novel, gives order to the data; he charts a map, in Mailer's metaphor, and that map is the novel each of us carries in his subconscious. We deal with the world on the basis of that novel, playing the roles the navigator tells us to, even when our raw data is acquired through faulty perception. Few of us are able to tell how or why our navigator operates as he does; in fact only the best writers are able to bring a little more of the nature of the navigator to consciousness and so become navigators themselves, directing the course of human life. Mailer seems to believe that the navigator holds the key to connecting the conscious and subconscious minds, or the past and the present, which he images as schizophrenic halves of what should be whole. Joining the schizophrenic portions of his own nature into a metaphor large enough to contain them is the process we see unfolding in *Advertisements*. By the end of the book Mailer has progressed far enough to have connected his past with his present, something Mikey Lovett, the amnesiac, was unable to do, and which is the crucial problem faced by the Sergius O'Shaugnessy of *The Deer Park*. This vital connection must be made before either Mailer or the America whose metaphorical hero he works at creating can move into the future with any coherent force. When Sam Slovoda sits down to write a long-contemplated novel he is stymied by his inability to create a hero who would give it shape:

> One could not have a hero today, Sam thinks, a man of action and contemplation, capable of sin, large enough for good, a man immense. There is only a modern hero damned by no more than the ugliness of wishes whose satisfaction he will never know. One needs a man who could walk the stage, someone who—no matter who, not himself. Someone, Sam thinks, who reasonably could not exist. (*Adv.*, p. 172)

The liberation of the self for union with the universal spirit which is the end of yoga is impossible for Sam because of his inability to conceive of a living hero.

The political articles which follow "The Man Who Studied Yoga" in *Advertisements* illustrate the need for Mailer to find a style appropriate to his developing ideas. In the *Partisan Review* symposium entitled "Our Country and Our Culture" in which he participated in 1952, he begins to articulate the need of the artist to oppose himself to the death-producing society, not to work from within the system (a position he was later to revise), and in 1954 in an article reviewing David Riesman's *Individualism Reconsidered*, Mailer aligns himself with the spirit of radicalism, while acknowledging the difficulty of maintaining it since it is "equivalent to accepting almost total intellectual alienation from America" (*Adv.*, p. 189). Such opposition does, however, give one a "clear sense of the enemy," and Mailer has consistently taken radical positions both in politics and in literature. To be a yea-sayer to things as they are is suicidal in Mailer's scheme of things, as it was in Melville's.

In an interview included in *Advertisements for Myself* Mailer describes himself as a "Marxian anarchist" who is less interested in "politics as politics" than "politics as a part of everything else in life" (*Adv.*, p. 253). The radical substance of his politics, from his 1948 campaigning for Henry Wallace through his 1969 campaign for mayor of New York on the interesting platform that the city become the fifty-first state, has not obscured the fact that he has tried to gain power through the established system. The methods of attaining and holding political power he would accept, it seems, while revolutionizing its end. In 1973, however, Mailer proposed the establishment of a powerful citizen's organization to be called the Fifth Estate, whose primary purpose was to have been to investigate conspiracies of national importance such as the political assassinations and Watergate which have been and are being kept secret from the public by the CIA and FBI. In this instance Mailer proposed an alternative to the system as a check on it.

The search for a style continues in the material included in part three of *Advertisements*, called "Births." This section is the most confessional of *Advertisements*, although in keeping with the rest of the book it is limited to the experiences which fostered Mailer's artistic growth. The particulars of his private life remain private unless they bear significantly on his work or illustrate some point, and if they do Mailer is surprisingly detached, frank, and undefensive of himself in their presentation, the result of his ability to view himself as a literary character. The somewhat banal piece, "The Homosexual Villain," for example, was the result of a conscious attempt to stop shying away from homosexuality as a subject, since it was to be explored in the eight-volume novel. Mailer acknowledges that the article was important to his growth, for he learned to dig "deep into the complex and often foul pots of thought where sex and society live in their murderous dialectic." Homosexuality also came to metaphorically represent for him "the endless twists of habit and defeat" which one must overcome to be "more of a man" (*Adv.*, p. 206). In addition, the essay reiterates the interrelationship in Mailer's view of artistic and personal growth and illustrates that his position is unconventionally moral:

> A writer has his talent, and for all one knows, he is born with it, but whether his talent develops is to some degree responsive to his use of it. He can grow as a person or he can shrink, and by this I don't intend any facile parallels between moral and artistic growth. The writer can become a bigger hoodlum if need be, but his alertness, his curiosity, his reaction to life must not diminish. The fatal thing is to shrink, to be interested in less, sympathetic to less, desiccating to the point where life itself loses its flavor, and one's passion for human understanding changes to weariness and distaste. (*Adv.*, pp. 208-9)

The end of the first half of *Advertisements* quite appropriately comes with the section on "The Last Draft of *The Deer Park*," for it marks a turning point in Mailer's career. When Rinehart refused to publish *The Deer Park* because Mailer would not edit a scene which obliquely involved fellatio, Mailer sent the book to eight other publishers before finding one who would accept it, G. P. Putnam. The ten weeks the book spent between publishers forced Mailer into a number of small confrontations which sapped him of the energy he had planned to devote to another novel. His vision of himself as one of the great writers of his generation collapsed, and he turned to the world of jazz and drugs, playing the role of a "psychic outlaw" (*Adv.*, p. 217). His new experiences convinced him that the style of *The Deer Park* was false, and he began to rework it. The problem centered around finding an appropriate style for his narrator, Sergius O'Shaugnessy. Mailer's recording of the emerging of Sergius's style is crucial:

> For six years I had been writing novels in the first person; it was the only way I could begin a book, even though the third person was more to my taste . . . the first person seemed to paralyze me, as if I had a horror of creating a voice which could be in any way bigger than myself. [Having gained self-confidence from his uncompromising position with Rinehart] for the first time I was able to use the first person in a way where I could suggest some of the stubbornness and belligerence I also might have, I was able to color the empty reality of that first person with some real feeling of how I had always felt. . . . I was able, then, to create an adventurer whom I believed in, and as he came alive for me, the other parts of the book . . . also came to life. . . . The most powerful leverage in fiction comes from point of view, and giving O'Shaugnessy courage gave passion to the others.
>
> . . . I was now creating a man who was braver and stronger than me, and the more my new style succeeded, the more I was writing an implicit portrait of myself as well. There is a shame in advertising yourself that way, a shame which became so strong that it was a psychological violation to go on. (*Adv.*, p. 220–21)

Mailer's problem, then, was that he could neither write about himself nor not write about himself. He had grown into someone worth writing about, but he had not yet gained the necessary detachment to consider himself as a literary character. Mailer pinpoints the central problem of the book: "In changing the young man, I saved the book from being minor, [I cannot agree that he did] but put a disproportion upon it because my narrator became too interesting, and not enough happened to him in the second half of the book" (*Adv.*, p. 226). A further problem of point of view in the novel, mentioned earlier, is that Sergius must imagine the dramatic scenes between Elena and Eitel at which he could not logically be present. "I have to wonder a little if I am the one to write about [the Eitel-Esposito affair]. Eitel is very different from me, and I do not know if I can find his style. Yet imagination becomes a vice if we do not exercise it," Sergius says in way of explanation (*DP*, p. 88).

His indecision as to whether Eitel's or his own story should have precedence is illustrated in this passage.

> [Eitel] told me his theory, and although I do not want to go into theory, maybe it is a part of character. I could write it today as he said it, and I think in all modesty I could even add a complexity or two, but this is partly a novel of how I felt at the time, and so I paraphrase as I heard it then, for it would take too long the other way. (*DP*, p. 106)

A further problem traceable to point of view is that Eitel's story is at least as interesting as that of Sergius, and while they complement each other structurally and thematically, they jar because of the manner in which each is told. The subdued narrative voice in the Eitel sections contrasted to the dominant one in the Sergius sections leaves the reader with a sense of imbalance. The book's real accomplishment as an entity, it may be argued, was to push back the frontier of sex in the serious novel.

The Deer Park was originally intended as part one of the eight-volume novel, with pleasure as its subject. It is certainly a central subject, but the exhortation issued by God at the novel's end, to "think of sex as Time, and Time as the connection of new circuits," is the significant message in terms of Mailer's work as a whole. Sex is a metaphor for either new connections and the hope that they will produce new life or for the dead-end self-seeking of lust. The search for new life is, after all, what brought the sick-spirited Sergius and Eitel to the imaginative Hell of Desert D'or where their courage was tested and in Eitel's case found wanting. Eitel is the failed artist figure. He espouses a theory similar to that in Matthew Arnold's poem, "The Buried Life," that each of us has a buried nature or "noble savage" which is "changed and whipped and trained by everything in life until it [is] almost dead." A mate with a similar buried nature may be found and they may help each other thrive, but their path is full of obstacles likely to defeat them (*DP*, 106-7). Eitel's theory not only is acted out in the course of his relationship with Elena; it also provides the skeleton of the plot for *An American Dream*. For Eitel defeat seems almost inevitable. Near the end of the novel, Sergius's experiences with

49

Mexican bullfighters illustrate what Eitel had never understood: "I was always most intrigued by the bullfighters who projected the most intense fear," Sergius records, "and then succeeded to put an imaginative fight together. The cowards know every way a man can fear the bull, and so on those rare days when they are able to dominate the movements of their bodies, they know more of the variations, and the moments when something new can be done" (*DP*, p. 299). A sense of fear, of the consequences of failure, can extract a better performance from a man. This is what to Mailer is an existential situation, where one acts despite his fear and grows or, like Eitel, gives in to fear and dies a little more. Mailer acknowledges his concern with "living in Hemingway's discipline," which means "that even if one dulled one's talents in the punishment of becoming a man, it was more important to be a man than a very good writer" (*Adv.*, p. 247), although of course for both men one cannot be a good writer without engaging in existential battles which can be mined for his writing. Sergius's survival of Hell, then, is dependent upon his comprehension of the reasons for Eitel's failure to survive. "I only am alone escaped to tell you," Sergius might have said, for like Ishmael or Mikey Lovett or the Mailer of *Advertisements for Myself*, he has been a participant-witness in a life-changing experience which it is his salvation to tell and the reader's to understand.

To Mailer, however, who at this point still measured a book's success by the number of copies it sold, *The Deer Park* was a failure. He had failed to convince others of the validity of his vision and so had to believe either that he "had no magic so great as to hasten the time of the apocalypse" or that the "wisdom, the reliability, and the authority of the public's literary mind" were at fault (*Adv.*, p. 231). He decided to appeal to an authority whose opinion he valued. When the copy of *The Deer Park* which he sent to Hemingway was returned unopened, Mailer moved one step closer to becoming his own critic.

The remainder of part three of *Advertisements for Myself* is devoted to Mailer's columns for *The Village Voice*. He had backed the paper financially from its inception in 1955 but had been too involved with *The Deer Park* to become interested in it. Following the publication of the novel, he described himself as

> anxious above all else to change a hundred self-defeating habits which locked my character into space too narrow for what I wanted to become, I was at the time like an actor looking for a rare role.... At heart, I wanted a war, and the Village was already glimpsed as the field for battle ... the column began as the declaration of my private war on American journalism, mass communications, and the totalitarianism of totally pleasant personality. (*Adv.*, pp. 258–59)

The *Village Voice* columns gave birth to a progression of ideas and stylistic explorations which culminated in "The White Negro." The military metaphor of the columns as battleground with General Mailer advancing upon the enemy is furthered by their defensive tone. In retrospect Mailer realizes that his rage "against that national conformity which smothered creativity" and "delayed the self-creation of the race" as well as against his own failings was untempered by the "fine conscious nets of restraint, caution, tact, elegance, taste, even [honorable] inhibition" which made for "good style" (p. 264). "By their inner history," Mailer concludes, "these columns are a debacle, because never before had I done so little where I committed so much" (*Adv.*, p. 265).

Mailer is very much concerned in these columns with his personal growth. In a manner characteristic of much of his earlier and all of his later work, he positions himself for an existential battle: a confrontation with an antithetical force in which what is most vital to both sides is laid on the line. His opposition in these columns, the social structure as he conceives of it, is of course an indifferent opponent, but this does not diminish his objective to purge it of its waste. Now imagery of purgation and waste is becoming characteristic of Mailer's writing. The artistic use of biological functions is important to his conception of the need to revitalize the human body and spirit, to invert the perversions of a death-producing society. Obscenity, for example, is presented in

51

one of the columns as a vital God-given means of expression which speeds the "true communication of soul to soul" and its suppression suppresses also the "creative spirit" (*Adv.*, p. 269).

Another of the columns' major concerns is with "truth." Mailer sees truth as Robert Browning did in *The Ring and the Book*, as the summary of the sentiments and actions of all those concerned with an event, which in turn creates other sentiments and actions. The artist has a special ability to imaginatively relate all of these "truths" into a whole. "The novelist trusts his 'vision'," Mailer tells us (*Adv.*, p. 281), and the reader is invited to as well. The importance of this concept to Mailer's future writing cannot be overestimated. It becomes both method and justification for his work from *The Armies of the Night* to *Marilyn*.

Another of the significant *Village Voice* columns is "The Hip and the Square," for in it Mailer begins to formulate his opposition to society into a metaphoric equivalent, the hipster and his style of life. This subject was the end of his exploratory columns; it provided a positive embodiment of his antisocial convictions and rebellious impulses. As Mailer begins to define it here, hip is

> an exploration into the nature of man [its] ultimate tendency . . . to return man to the center of the universe rather than to continue his reduction into less and less of a biochemical mechanism . . . Hip is an American existentialism . . . based on a mysticism of the flesh, and its origins can be traced back into the instinctive apprehension and appreciation of existence which one finds in the Negro and the soldier, in the criminal psychopath and the dope addict and jazz musician, in the prostitute, in the actor, in the—if one can visualize such a possibility—in the marriage of the call-girl and the psychoanalyst. . . . It is a language to describe states of being which is as yet without its philosophical dictionary.
>   . . . Hip with its special and intense awareness of the present tense of life . . . has a view of life which is predicated on growth and the nuances[21] of growth. (*Adv.*, pp. 292–93)

The claims Mailer makes for hip in this early expository essay are to be explored more fully in the work which follows, culminating in their fictional presentation in *An American Dream*. The hipster becomes for Mailer the agent for change, for bringing about the revolution of consciousness which he believes vital to the nation's survival. A revolution is violent by nature, and yet Mailer believes, as he states in his final column for *The Village Voice*, that "violence is better without than within, better as individual actions than as the collective murders of society, and if we have courage enough there is beauty beneath" (*Adv.*, p. 303).

Part four of *Advertisements for Myself*, entitled "Hipsters," contains the powerfully provocative essay, "The White Negro." In the "Sixth Advertisement For Myself" which precedes that essay, Mailer indicates that circumstances forced him "to begin the trip into the psychic wild of 'The White Negro' " and that the experience resulted in "one of the best things" he has done (*Adv.*, p. 310). We are not given the details of the self-exploration that produced the essay, because Mailer believes that a factual account would strip him of the power "to project the best of one's imagination out into a creative space larger than the items of one's life" (ibid.). We are reminded that Mailer up to this point views his past self as he would a fictional character. He stresses that from this point on, however, he is not sufficiently detached from the events of his life to report them to us. Here the book takes a new turn; we are informed that "The White Negro," "The Time of Her Time," and "Advertisements for Myself on the Way Out" are the "seeds" which give the book its significance. In a metaphor of creation, Mailer tells us that "seed" is "the end of the potentialities seen for oneself, and every organism creates its seed out of the experience of its past and its unspoken vision or curse upon the future" (ibid.). Seed, then, is the link between past, present, and future.

The first of these seeds, "The White Negro," was published as a separate work in 1957 but did not receive much attention until included in *Advertisements for Myself*. Reviewers tended to seize upon "The White Negro" as the core of the book and in fact to ignore or slight most of the other material.[22] The essay is certainly the ideological core of *Ad-*

vertisements and a considerable stylistic advance over earlier essays. However, the reason for the critical attention it received was that it advocated the violent overthrow of the American system—social, economic, and political. The essay was labeled irresponsible, dangerous, and insane. Attempts were made to dominate it intellectually, an approach Mailer had ridiculed in "The Man Who Studied Yoga." Those who sincerely attacked the essay's ideas, however, must have believed with Mailer that a man's writing can cause significant action by others. They were right by Mailer's standards to oppose what they considered profoundly dangerous. For Mailer, such an antithetical attack was a necessary step in promoting his ideas. The defeat of a worthy opponent can bring new vigor to one's cause. F. W. Dupee correctly perceived the dialectical nature of hip, but imputed it to Mailer's inability to handle his material. To Dupee, Mailer "over-formulates Hip, schematizes it, makes its way and words merely antithetical to those of its enemy the Square."[23] Likewise, Edmund Fuller notes that one is either a hipster or a square and questions whether there are any in-betweens in Mailer's work.[24]

While much attention was paid the ideas, to my knowledge no one has noted the insidiousness of the form in which they are presented in "The White Negro." It is that of a formal essay, complete with epigraph, division into sections, and quotations from authoritative sources. The careful progression from a statement with which all must agree, that is, that concentration camps were the result of the action of a totalitarian state, to the assumption that death is the end of all actions by societies, has been overlooked as has the presentation of opinion as fact, and the loaded language calculated to produce a given response—all standard techniques of propaganda.

Mailer establishes in the essay's first section that individualism has been a casualty of the Second World War, and that man must live with the fact of his death by deus ex machina rather than as a consequence of his actions. The remainder of the essay is devoted to a description of the hip-

ster, the antithesis to the movement of the age. Mailer now
begins to create the myth of the hipster, who embodies not
only the radical impulses in Mailer himself but also those of
Natty Bumppo and his descendants. The hipster is one with
the mythic American hero whose "essential nature" Lawrence described as "hard, isolate, stoic, and a killer."[25]

In Mailer's schematism the hipster is an "American existentialist" who lives with the imminence of death, isolates
himself from society, explores "the rebellious imperative of
the self," and exhibits extraordinary courage. His intellectual antecedents Mailer traces to Lawrence, Henry Miller, Wilhelm Reich, and Hemingway; his embodiment to the *mén-
age à trois* of the bohemian, the juvenile delinquent, and the
Negro through the mediums of drugs and jazz. The White
Negro is the synthesis of these various impulses. What that
synthesis means ultimately to Mailer is revealed in the following passage:

> incompatibles have come to bed, the inner life and the violent life,
> the orgy and the dream of love, the desire to murder and the desire to
> create, a dialectical conception of existence with a lust for power, a
> dark, romantic, and yet undeniably dynamic view of existence for it
> sees every man and woman as moving individually through each
> moment of life forward into growth or backward into death. (*Adv.*, p.
> 316)

By bringing the buried self to consciousness, hip enables
one to grow toward wholeness. The schematizing of hip is
thus an important stage in Mailer's development. Like his
creator, the hipster is a navigator engaged in "codifying . . .
the suppositions on which his inner universe is constructed" (ibid.). He accomplishes this through self-analysis, "for
if one is to change one's habits, one must go back to the
source of their creation." He "seeks to find those violent parallels to the violent and often hopeless contradictions he
knew as an infant and as a child," and "if he has the
courage to meet the parallel situation at the moment when
he is ready, then he has a chance to act as he has never acted before . . . and so free himself to remake a bit of his nervous system" (*Adv.*, p. 320). This commonly accepted psy-

55

chological concept, that one rids oneself of unhealthy repressions by acting them out, is the groundwork for the provocative concept which follows: that the commission of murder may be necessary and indeed courageous to purge oneself of violence in order to leave oneself open for love. The extremity of contemporary man's condition requires extreme action in Mailer's view, and the logic of his presentation requires us either to accept or to reject his thesis in full.

Few readers or critics have found this advocation of violence tolerable in Mailer. Most recently a young novelist, Alan Lelchuk, has followed the theory to its inevitable extreme, when in *American Mischief* a young Raskolnikovian revolutionary shoots Mailer in what he conceived as the ultimate existential act: to free himself even of his dependence upon his hero.[26] I would contend that the theory of violence expressed in "The White Negro" is to be taken metaphorically rather than literally, as is the case in *An American Dream* where a murder precipitates a rebirth for the protagonist. While it is true, as some would counter, that Mailer stabbed his second wife, Adele Morales, during a party at his home in 1960, we cannot connect the theory with the act, since we cannot know Mailer's motivations at the time. As a final point, it might be said that Mailer has discovered in the sixteen years since "The White Negro" alternate means for the individual to free himself from the destructive network of society, as we shall see.

Love for the White Negro is "the search for an orgasm more apocalyptic than the one which preceded it" (*Adv.*, p. 321). By orgasm Mailer seems to mean an intense moment in which a little more of the mystery of the self is revealed to him. The "IT" which Lawrence speaks of, the fulfillment of which brings true liberty, may have been in Mailer's mind when he wrote the following:

> to be with it is to have grace, is to be closer to the secrets of that inner unconscious life which will nourish you if you can hear it, for you are then nearer to that God which every hipster believes is located in the senses of his body, that trapped, mutilated and nonetheless megalomaniacal God who is It, who is energy, life, sex, force, the Yoga's *pra-*

56

na, the Reichian's orgone, Lawrence's "blood," Hemingway's "good," the Shavian life-force; "It"; God; not the God of the churches but the unachievable whisper of mystery within the sex, the paradise of limitless energy and perception just beyond the next wave of the next orgasm. (*Adv.*, pp. 324–25)

If paradise lies in "limitless energy and perception," each good orgasm brings a glimpse of it and provides faith in its existence. The apocalyptic orgasm that Mailer envisions as the end of the hipster's search is a state of being in which the mysteries of existence would be perpetually unfolded. This concept of Revelations is not remote from the Christian one. Mailer rejects the atheism of some European existentialists in favor of this vision of "the possibilities within death" opened by an intensified consciousness (*Adv.*, p. 316).

A secular corollary to the insight obtained through the good orgasm is that of the character and his context. In hip, the context (by which I believe Mailer means all the nuances of a given situation) dominates the individual, "because his character is less significant than the context in which he must function." Each person is "not only his character but his context, since the success or failure of an action in a given context reacts upon the character and therefore affects what the character will be in the next context. What dominates both character and context is the energy available at the moment of intense conflict" (*Adv.*, p. 327). Experience is thus cumulative, a line of movement but also a series of units. The idea is common enough and is present in Mailer's own work from its beginnings. It gains importance, however, from its central position in the existentialist philosophy which dominates all of Mailer's later work. Character in such a philosophy is "perpetually ambivalent and dynamic" and enters into "an absolute relativity where there are no truths other than the isolated truths of what each observer feels at each instant of his existence" (ibid.). This concept relates to that of the expansion of the self through bringing to consciousness diverse and hitherto unexplored aspects of the self.

"The White Negro" concludes with a vision of the nature

of society having been acted upon by hip as a "gigantic synthesis of human action" in which we come to understand what leads to "our creation and disasters, our growth, our attrition, and our rebellion" (*Adv.*, p. 331). The difficulty of disagreeing with the desirability of this end lends strength to the essay. Despite some unevenness and a tendency toward vagueness, Mailer's "radical humanism" gains powerful expression in this essay. Self-confidence replaces defensiveness in the tone, an indication of the growing assurance of Mailer's style as he explores ideas which excite him with a sense of direction. The essay stands in relation to *Advertisements for Myself* as *Advertisements* does to his work as a whole: it is the culmination both stylistically and intellectually of a phase of Mailer's growth, encompassing his past work and leading toward that in the future.

The debate and interview which follow "The White Negro" in the collection explore the philosophy of hip somewhat further. Each is a dialectical exchange, a form which Mailer favors as a means of keeping him on his toes as well as giving him "a clear sense of the enemy." "Reflections on Hip" consists of an exchange of views with Jean Malaquais and Ned Polsky. Mailer is more specific in discussing the nature of the hip revolution. He sees it as "moving not forward toward action and more equitable distribution [as the Marxist revolution was to do], but backward toward being and the secrets of human energy" (*Adv.*, p. 336). Instinct is to dominate consciousness in this neoprimitive state he envisions, and he believes that human nature is basically good and creative. He reiterates that we must develop through dialectics a view of man which embraces all contradictions. This concept as the end product of human growth relates Mailer to the humanists.

An interview in 1958 with Richard G. Stern, called "Hip, Hell and the Navigator," ends part four of *Advertisements for Myself*. Stern's penetrating opening question asks whether Mailer advocates hip or is simply describing a phenomenon. Mailer sidesteps the question, but his subsequent answers reveal, as do all of his writings on hip, that

58

he is instead creating a mythology which has little factual basis. He compares the hipster's "state of extreme awareness" with the novelist's ability to "illumine each line of his work with the greatest intensity of experience" (p. 350). So experience and expression are linked, and one writes more about a few experiences in order to express their "nuances." In this way hip "opens the possibility that the novel, along with many other art forms, may be growing into something larger rather than something smaller" (p. 352). Other claims made for hip in this interview are that it gives meaning and morality to our actions; that our actions are good or evil as our senses and instincts inform us (another outgrowth of Hemingway's code); and that hip, in fact, is a religion in which man's fate is dependent upon God's fate and vice versa. What this interview reveals is that Mailer's mythology of hip has cosmic proportions, and that he has for the first time developed a vision large enough to give direction and room for growth to himself both as a man and an artist who wishes to save himself and his society from a painful and progressive death.

A mythology may be described as a system for explaining and ordering phenomena concerning human relationships with nature, the supernatural, and other human beings, and this is precisely what Mailer has formulated as hip by the end of part four of *Advertisements*. With certain adaptations, this mythology gives structure to his vision up to the present.

In part five, "Games and Ends," Mailer continues to define his mythology and its antithesis, here imaged as the "Wasp" way of life ("cancer has been their last contribution to civilization" [p. 357]) against which hip must wage war. Robert A. Bone accuses Mailer of arrested development, claiming that hip is an outgrowth of Mailer's war experience and that it is "a symptom, not a cure for our malaise."[27] World War II surely confirmed Mailer's sense of the dialectical nature of things, but the earlier study of Marx laid the foundation for his thinking. The war metaphors which Mailer uses throughout *Advertisements for Myself*, as well as numerous other works, are a vital part of Mailer's "embattled vision," to borrow a phrase from Norman Podhoretz,[28] and in that vision there is, for him, as much at stake as in Milton's vision of the war between God and Satan for possession of the universe.

The advertisement for part five makes use of a war metaphor. Mailer divides the remainder of the book into three sections: the first a "restcamp" after the "patrol" through "The White Negro"; the second a "reconnaissance" into "another difficult terrain"; and the third a "forced march on the mind" (*Adv.*, p. 359). The first two parts being a potpourri, we shall be concerned only with the latter. This final section of the book opens with the "Last Advertisement For Myself Before the Way Out," from which I quoted at length in the introduction. It is here that Mailer reviews with bitterness the wasted talents of his and Hemingway's generations, castigates himself for his own failures, and ends on the hopeful note that the novel with which he currently is engaged will carry what the great writers have told us "another part of the way" (*Adv.*, p. 439). Aside from two short introductory comments, this is the last we hear of the authorial voice in *Advertisements for Myself*. The "Last Advertisement" reiterates Mailer's shifting dependence from early models and public opinion to himself. He knows he is not yet the hero America needs to unite itself ("I am still at this formal middle of my life a creator of sentiments larger than my work"), but he has delineated one in the form of the hipster, who, until he proves inadequate, metaphorically contains the elements Mailer believes can revitalize America. In his diagnosis of America's sickness and his prescriptions for recovery, Mailer is out of step with his own generation of writers, most of whom describe futile attempts by their protagonists to break out of the patterns woven by their pasts or at best the ironic attainment of a freedom they are not equipped to handle. The list of these writers is long and impressive and includes Bellow, Malamud, Updike, Roth, Baldwin. They are descendants of those American writers whom R. W. B. Lewis has grouped in "The Party of

Irony,"[29] while Mailer synthesizes in himself the concerns both of the party of irony and the party of hope: he does not merely long for a new Eden but actively seeks it through whatever means are available to him.

Having led us along the winding spiral of his career, Mailer stakes the continuance of his progress as an artist on the three remaining pieces of *Advertisements for Myself*, parts of the projected novel calculated to be "the longest ball ever to go up into the accelerated hurricane air of our American letters." Although that novel was never completed, the three pieces are of interest in ascertaining the direction Mailer expected his work to take following *Advertisements* and his growing self-confidence in it, won through the struggle with the enemy in himself whose defeat is the subject of *Advertisements*.

"The Time of Her Time" is a long story which may stand independent of the novel which was to contain it, more so than "The Man Who Studied Yoga." Interestingly, the story was omitted from the British edition of *Advertisements*, undoubtedly because of its sexual explicitness.[30] The narrator is the Sergius O'Shaugnessy we glimpse at the end of *The Deer Park*, who, having learned from the bullfighters how to dominate fear and open the possibilities for growth, has opened his own "Escuela de Torear" in Greenwich Village.

The numerical symbology of the opening pages prepares for the orgasmic apocalypse which is the story's object. Sergius's room is one hundred feet long (the perfect whole), with nineteen windows on three of the walls and part of the fourth (potentially apocalyptic); twelve (the apocalyptic number) and divisions of it appear. Further, it is in spring that Sergius and Denise meet and on the third occasion of their lovemaking that Denise reaches her first orgasm through intercourse. Their sexual engagements are imaged as battles each wages on the body of the other for the victory of his style of life. Sergius is an existentialist qualified to instruct Denise in the art of living, while she is a Jewish liberal pseudointellectual, a victim of psychoanalysis. She is also the "Jewish college girl from Brooklyn with a Master's degree" included as one of Sergius's bullfight students in *The Deer Park* (p. 301). The magnitude of the battle is evidenced by Sergius's feeling that victory, that is, bringing Denise to orgasm, "would add to the panoplies of my ego some peculiar (but for me, valid) ingestion of her arrogance, her stubborness, and her will—those necessary ingredients of which I could not yet have enough for my own ambitions." Defeat, on the other hand, would bring him "closer to a general depression, a fog bank of dissatisfaction with [him]self" (*Adv.*, p. 458), the familiar grow or pay theme in Mailer. Although Denise cannot as fully appreciate the nuances of the situation as Sergius can, it is clear that she knows that if her masculine, agressive will can be feminized by achieving orgasm, she will then enter "the time of her Time" when body, mind, and will are in phase with one another. What finally separates Denise from her past and gives her the terrifying freedom for which she hates Sergius are the whispered words which bring her to climax: "You dirty little Jew" (*Adv.*, p. 464), a sentence full of Maileristic nuances. And in a parting shot at his masculinity, Denise becomes in Sergius's eyes "a hero fit for me" (p. 465).

The second half of the story moves with a rhythm of its own; it is the work of a mature, self-confident artist. As Howard Harper has perceptively remarked of the story's style:

> [Mailer] has moved to a new synthesis of rhythm, sound, and emotional tones and overtones. The words are loaded with emotional as well as literal meaning, and with their vivid evocations of sounds, smells, tactile feelings, and motions—as well as the more conventional visual images—Mailer achieves an almost overwhelming sense of the psychological totality of his situation.[31]

"The Time of Her Time," then, achieves on a small scale what Mailer wishes to accomplish on a grand scale. The two remaining pieces depend more heavily on the context of the projected novel in which they were to be included than "The Time of Her Time." One, the poem "Dead Ends," treats the theme of the cancerous waste of narcissism and homosexuality in a form different from others in which Mailer has expressed similar ideas. However much he rails against jargon of any kind, which he considers mechanistic, this poem suffers from a concentrated overdose of his own jargon.[32]

It is significant that *Advertisements for Myself* ends with a beginning: the "Prologue to a Long Novel" entitled "Advertisements for Myself on the Way Out." From the title alone it is clear that Mailer considers his new novel to be an outgrowth of the book he ends with this piece. The prologue is a fictional summation of the style of life and art which Mailer has worked up to in *Advertisements*. It is told by a first-person narrator resembling the navigator who writes the novel of our subconscious minds. The character of the navigator cannot be pinned down; like the Devil, he can assume all shapes and, like God, he is all-knowing. The narrator also theorizes about time, a concept of great significance to Mailer since *The Deer Park*. Time is seen here as growth, as the "natural unwinding" of a spiral, as the connections forged in human relationships. Time is either potential or dynamic, and each individual follows his own time spiral. As with his concept of God, Mailer makes time wholly dependent upon human action.

Marion Faye appears to be the novel's hero, and like a true Mailer hero Faye is characterized as "Napoleonic" in ambition, "wide as the Renaissance" in talents, with "instincts about the nature of growth, a lover's sense of the moment of crisis, [knowing,] perhaps as well as anyone alive, how costly is defeat when it is not soothed by greater consciousness, and how wasteful is the profit of victory when there is not the courage to employ it" (*Adv.*, p. 476). Marion has reached a crucial moment in his life, a typically extreme situation in Mailer: he must decide to murder a former friend or to wither away by stifling the desire. (It is, of course, the situation which faces Stephen Rojack at the beginning of *An American Dream*.)

The action of the novel is to derive from a gathering of people of all types in Faye's gothic Provincetown home where murder, suicide, and orgy are to engage them and the reader in the most vital mysteries of the self. As projected, the novel is most ambitious, the style of the narration is as "self-consciously attractive and formal" (*Adv.*, p. 219) as the first draft of *The Deer Park*, and perhaps it is well that Mailer abandoned the book. It would surely have occupied all of his middle years, and he would probably have outgrown it before it was completed. And yet its very ambitiousness is proof of Mailer's victory over his defeats and frustrations. Like the young man who wished to write *the* novel of World War II, Mailer still aims for the gold medal, but, as we have seen, his motives and ends have grown tremendously in these years. Thus, *Advertisements for Myself* brings to a conclusion the first important phase of Mailer's career. It is a dramatic account of the manner in which the man and the style come together, and of the potential released by the synthesis.

NOTES

1. Marvin Mudrick, "Mailer and Styron," p. 361.
2. Barry H. Leeds, *The Structured Vision of Norman Mailer*, p. 224.
3. Robert W. Lawler, "Norman Mailer," p. 86.
4. Paul Carroll, "*Playboy* Interview," p. 72.
5. Cf. Norman Mailer, *The Naked and the Dead*, p. 443 (all further references are cited in the text, and the title will be abbreviated to *ND*); *Adv.*, pp. 389, 425, 476; Carroll, "*Playboy* Interview," p. 72.
6. According to J. E. Cirlot's *A Dictionary of Symbols*, the spiral traditionally is "a symbol of growth," is "essentially macrocosmic," is an attribute of power, and "may symbolize the relationship between the circle and the centre. For the spiral is associated with the idea of the dance, and especially with primitive dances of healing and incantation, when the pattern of movement develops as a spiral curve. Such spiral movements . . . may be regarded as figures intended to induce a state of ecstasy and to enable man to escape from the material world and to enter the beyond, through the 'hole' symbolized by the mystic Centre" (pp. 290–92).
7. In his perception of the curve as trajectory, as "the upward leap of a culture [which] is blunted, slowed, brought to its early doom" (*ND*, p. 444), and his obsessive desire to pursue its mystery and to "mold the curve," Cummings's prototype is Ahab.
8. Norman Mailer, *The Deer Park*, p. 318. All further references are cited in the text, and the title will be abbreviated to *DP*.
9. Wayne C. Booth, *The Rhetoric of Fiction*, pp. 149–65.

10. Richard Foster, *Norman Mailer*, p. 26.
11. Cf. John W. Aldridge, *After the Lost Generation*, pp. 135–36; Willard Thorp, *American Writing in the Twentieth Century*, p. 146; and John M. Muste, "Norman Mailer and John Dos Passos," pp. 361–74, among others.
12. Cf. Ihab Hassan, *Radical Innocence*, p. 141; and Walter B. Rideout, *The Radical Novel in the United States*, pp. 270–73, among others.
13. See my *Norman Mailer: A Comprehensive Bibliography* for a list of these.
14. John Stark, "*Barbary Shore*," p. 407.
15. Cf. Max F. Schulz's discussion of *Barbary Shore* as a modern *Purgatorio* in *Radical Sophistication*, pp. 73–81.
16. Leeds, *The Structured Vision of Norman Mailer*, pp. 66–67.
17. Norman Mailer, *Barbary Shore*, p. 223. All further references are cited in the text, and the title will be abbreviated to *BS*.
18. After my original draft was written, I discovered that John Stark has noted even more extensive similarities between the two books. See Stark, *Barbary Shore*, pp. 403–4.
19. Leeds, *The Structured Vision of Norman Mailer*, pp. 66–67.
20. Norman Mailer, "Some Dirt in the Talk," pp. 265–66.
21. "Nuances" was originally misprinted as "nuisances," an error preserved with explanation in Mailer's text.
22. Cf. the following: Robert A. Bone, "Private Mailer Re-enlists," pp. 389–94; Paul Breslow, "The Hipster and the Radical," pp. 102–5; Stuart Hampshire, "Mailer United," pp. 515–16.
23. F. W. Dupee, "The American Norman Mailer," p. 131.
24. Edmund Fuller, *Man in Modern Fiction*, p. 160.
25. D. H. Lawrence, *Studies in Classic American Literature*, p. 62.
26. Pp. 279–97. Mailer threatened to sue Lelchuk for depicting him as "dying with his pants down," for in the original version of the novel Mailer is shot through the anus. In Lelchuk's published version Mailer gets it in the end but fights back.
27. Bone, "Private Mailer Re-enlists," p. 394.
28. Norman Podhoretz, "Norman Mailer," pp. 185–202.
29. R. W. B. Lewis, *The American Adam*, p. 7.
30. Hampshire, "Mailer United," p. 515.
31. Howard M. Harper, Jr., *Desperate Faith*, pp. 118–19.
32. The poem defines the cancer metaphor through a dialogue between a first-person protagonist and his host (double entendre intended, no doubt). The language is heavy, abstract, and stilted for the most part, in the manner of bad Shelley or Byron.

> *In the logic of retreat*, said I even louder,
> *when the body and mind are sick*
> *(in their cups of*
> *cowardice and despair and defeat*
> *and hatred which never breathed*
> *the air of open rage)*

EXISTENTIAL BATTLES

> then we are left only to choose our disease
>   for by the sick of logic
>   the choice is closed to suffer
>   psychosis
>   that the insanity from which we flee
>   will not hunt the boredom of our cells
>   into the arms
>   of the arch-narcissist
>   our lover, the devil,
>   whose ego is iron
>   and never flags
>   in its wild respect
>   for cool power.

(Adv., p. 468)

2

PHASE TWO:
AN AMERICAN DREAM

Mailer's growth in the period following
the publication of *Advertisements for
Myself* to the appearance of the final version of *An American Dream* in 1965 may be characterized as that from young
adulthood to full maturity. Personal and artistic failures
marred the years from late 1959 to 1962. Seemingly testing
the theory of violence developed in "The White Negro,"
Mailer stabbed his second wife, Adele Morales, at a party
held to celebrate his candidacy for the mayoralty of New
York in 1960. Committed to Bellevue Hospital, Mailer made
an eloquent plea for his own sanity and was released. The
incident left its scars, however, and of course ended for the
time his political ambitions. A book of poems published in
1962, *Deaths for the Ladies (and other disasters)*, proved
aptly named. Neither the themes nor the forms of these poems were significant advances beyond what Mailer had already accomplished in *Advertisements for Myself*, although
the book has merit if only because it represents another of
Mailer's incursions into unknown territory.

In an introduction written for the reissuance of *Deaths for
the Ladies* in 1971, Mailer notes that the poems were written
at a time when he could do no other work and was worried
about becoming an alcoholic. He had been writing poems
now and then for years: his miscellanies *The Presidential
Papers* and *Cannibals and Christians* are interspersed with
them, but *Deaths for the Ladies* represents his only real

67

effort to enter the arena as a poet. The book received a few reviews, none more uncomplimentary than that in *Time*,[1] which Mailer tells us inspired him to "go out to war again, and try to hew huge strokes with the only broadsword God ever gave [one], a glimpse of something like Almighty prose."[2] He knows that his "gifts as a poet were determined to be small," but he feels that the book offers an innovation: "It was a movie in words. I set it with the greatest care. . . . The spaces were chosen with much deliberation, the repetitions of phrases were like images in a film. The music of the poem as a whole—if it had any—was like the montage of a film" (*Deaths*, p. 3). These remarks will be of interest in tracing the evolution of Mailer's thoughts on film, something I shall deal with later. The poems are interconnected by theme and by repetition of all or parts of certain of them, such as "Explanations" which reminds us that

> The art of
> the
> short hair
> is that
> it
> don't
> go on
> for
> too long.

(*Deaths*, [unpaginated])

which may be taken as the poem's chief virtue. Some, however, are witty, others anticipate themes to be explored in future prose, and a few are concerned with the forms and aims of poetry, as is this one:

> Prose
> can pass
> into
> poetry
> when
> its heart
> is intense

```
For one
    can then
        dispense
        with whence
            went
                the verse.
Rhythm
    and rhyme
    may mask
        the movements
            of time.
                Remember
            that the sound
                of time
is flesh.
```

(Deaths, [unpaginated])

Deaths for the Ladies is valuable to students of Mailer, if not of poetry, for what it reveals of his themes and techniques in this genre.

Much of Mailer's writing during this period was to be found in magazines, including a monthly column for *Esquire* from November 1962 to December 1963 entitled "The Big Bite." Some of these columns and other magazine pieces were collected as *The Presidential Papers*, published in 1963. I will write more of this volume later. Late in 1963 Mailer began work on *An American Dream*, and it occupied the center of his attention through 1965.

In *Advertisements for Myself* Mailer had announced that he "would try to hit the longest ball ever to go up into the accelerated hurricane air of our American letters." The long novel he then envisioned as "the longest ball" he set aside in 1963 to begin work on *An American Dream*. The significance Mailer attached to that novel may be seen in a passage from *Cannibals and Christians* which I quoted in the introduction. What America needed, Mailer argued, was a "single great work which would clarify a nation's vision of itself" in the manner of Tolstoy and Stendhal. Dreiser tried and failed, presumably coming close in *An American Tragedy*, and since then, Mailer charged, the novelist's vision has been partial, a microcosm contained in a metaphor, rather than "a creation equal to the phenomenon of the country itself" (*CC*, p. 99). Even Hemingway and Faulkner "had given up trying to do it all" (ibid.). The magnum opus which Mailer intended to write, one may conclude, was to be the nation's as well as his own. To a practical mind the immensity of Mailer's ambition seems self-defeating if not absurdly grandiose. And yet *An American Dream* is surely among those American novels from the Leatherstocking tales to *Absalom! Absalom!* which help to clarify our vision of our national self both past and present, ideally and realistically. I will argue that Mailer's novel has significantly enlarged the literature of the American Dream in both form and substance.

If one may gauge the force of a novel by the quantity of criticism it provokes, *An American Dream* is easily Mailer's most powerful book to date. While most criticism of it has been either favorable with reservations or extremely condemnatory, the growing number of Mailer scholars find deep significance in the novel. As one such critic has expressed it, *An American Dream* "aims at fictions's ultimate virtue: the rendering of the uncommunicable."[3]

It is his vision of the uncommunicable dream-life of the nation in the middle of the twentieth century that Mailer has rendered in *An American Dream*. The novel's title suggests that its substance is a version of the central myth in American literature, that of the dream of forsaking past corruptions to begin life anew, to *make* a new life in a new place. Few of America's major novelists have not recorded the failure of that dream for whatever reasons they envision: the inherent evil in man, the encroachment of the machine and "civilization"; few have found the dream compatible with experience. Typically the American hero either lights out for the territory or is forced to compromise his expectations through an early death, madness, or a bitter old age. The American experience as recorded by our best novelists kills innocence and leaves in its place an aching sense of loss insufficiently soothed by the wisdom gained from the experience. Perhaps Mailer alone of our contemporary novelists has a vision of America's descent into the "heart of darkness," of its grappling with the Devil, and of its emergence with a sense of fresh possibility gained from this most elemental battle. He seems to be saying, America has long known how to murder, let her now learn how to create. In addition to rendering the past and present American experience, Mailer offers an imaginative possibility for the future, *an* American Dream offered in place of what has become *the* American Dream. In terms of Northrop Frye's cycle of myths, Mailer steps from the antiheroic ironic literary mode of his contemporaries to begin a new cycle in the mythic-cum-romantic mode in which gods play a part and the hero is a human being who "moves in a world in which the ordinary laws of nature are slightly suspended."[4]

Mailer presented his conception of the American Dream in conventional terms in "Superman Comes to the Supermarket," retitled "The Existential Hero" for *The Presidential Papers*. "We have used up our frontier," he tells us, "but the psychological frontier . . . is still alive with untouched possibilities and dire unhappy all-but-lost opportunities." Typically he sees these possibilities in terms of combat. American politics have had "little to do with the real subterranean life of America," Mailer asserts, so that an "army which would dare to enter the valley in force might not only determine a few new political formations, but indeed could create more politics itself" (*PP*, p. 37). In other words, politics, like American life generally, has ceased to be adventurous, failed to absorb the psychological changes which have occurred over the years. I quote again the passage from this essay which could serve as the epigraph to *An American Dream*:

> Since the First World War Americans have been leading a double life, and our history has moved on two rivers, one visible, the other underground; there has been the history of politics which is concrete, factual, practical and unbelievably dull if not for the consequences of the actions of some of these men; and there is a subterranean river of untapped ferocious, lonely and romantic desires, that concentration of ecstasy and violence which is the dream life of the nation. (*PP*, p. 51)

71

A fall took place in our century "from individual to mass man," and America was more vulnerable to "homogenization" than Europe because she was comparably rootless. "Yet," Mailer goes on,

> America was also the country in which the dynamic myth of the Renaissance—that every man was potentially extraordinary—knew its most passionate persistence. Simply, America was the land where people still believed in heroes. . . . It was a country which had grown by the leap of one hero past another. . . . And when the West was filled, the expansion turned inward, became part of an agitated, over-excited, superheated dream life. The film studios threw up their searchlights as the frontier was finally sealed, and the romantic possibilities of the old conquest of land turned into a vertical myth, trapped within the skull, of a new kind of heroic life. . . . And this myth, that each of us was born to be free, to wander, to have adventure, and to grow on the waves of the violent, the perfumed, and the unexpected, had a force which could not be tamed . . . it was as if the message in the labyrinth of the genes would insist that violence was locked with creativity, and adventure was the secret of love. (*PP*, pp. 52-53)

Over the years, Mailer theorizes, politics and the myth, or the reality and the dream, had hopelessly diverged. What was needed to reunite them was a hero to embody the whole life of the nation (cf. Introduction, pp. 21-22). Should such a hero be lacking, the result would be "a totalitarianism of the psyche by the stultifying techniques of the mass media" (*PP*, p. 57) and eventually national death through destruction from within and without, America's enemies taking advantage of her weakness.

The essay establishes the hope that John Kennedy would be such a hero; the book itself is a testament to Kennedy's failure to measure up to Mailer's conception of him, both in life and because of death. *The Presidential Papers* were written as a kind of Renaissance didactic manual to refine the inherently noble qualities in those who were to hold the reins of power, for the powerful attract the attention of the gods, Mailer believes. "Ultimately a hero is a man who would argue with the gods, and so awaken devils to contest his vision. The more a man can achieve, the more he may be certain that the devil will inhabit a part of his creation," he contends (*PP*, p. 8).

An American Dream

Mailer's vision of American possibility takes its inception, then, from two historical periods, both of which were uniquely vital and creative ages when the limits of human possibility were explored: the Renaissance and America before the closing of the frontier. It is Mailer's belief that such an age is possible again in America provided that she finds a hero with wit, passion, and grace whose life the nation may image.

In the opening pages of *An American Dream*, we are presented with the current version of the American Dream, transmogrified from its original Edenic associations through the late nineteenth-century postfrontier vertical myth presented in the Horatio Alger novels: that hard work, clean living, and a pinch of luck are all one needs in a land of opportunity—provided that one is a Wasp—to move up the ladder of success toward wealth and power. What is more likely in modern America is the attainment of wealth and power not through one's own efforts but through association by marriage or inheritance. Stephen Richards Rojack equates himself with John F. Kennedy because both have arrived at their positions through two similar routes. One is the ladder of success of the Harvard-educated war hero turned congressman, the other route by association with wealth and power: Kennedy through inheritance and Rojack through marriage to Deborah Caughlin Mangarvidi Kelly, whose ancestry denotes the melting-pot metaphor of America itself. Kennedy had continued along the obvious lines of the transmogrified Horatio Alger myth, that any rich son of a Catholic immigrant has a chance to be president of the United States. Mailer had already argued in *The Presidential Papers* that Kennedy's brand of heroism was lacking a vital ingredient: the imaginative power to act as a catalyst to unite the subterranean America with the conventional one. His purpose in thus establishing Rojack's similarities to Kennedy is to emphasize this crucial difference, to propose Rojack as a possible hero and through the act of writing the novel to attempt to *make* him a surrogate hero for the failed Kennedy and for Mailer himself. The novel in this light may be considered a growth experience for its au-

73

thor as well as a vision of the possibilities for growth for the nation itself.

Rojack is established from the beginning of the novel as an existentialist whose essential difference from Kennedy is that he has a sense of the abyss, of "magic, dread, and the perception of death" as "the roots of motivation,"[5] whereas Kennedy in all probability "never saw the abyss" (*AAD*, p. 10). Mailer's sense of the possibility for heroism in *Advertisements for Myself*, it will be remembered, lay in the hipster. As has been seen in *The Presidential Papers*, however, Mailer came to believe that America needed a hero who could lead a whole nation, not a divided one, a hero with a face and a personality to personify the "large historic ideas" which come to power (*PP*, p. 16), a hero out in the open who could bring the enemy out in the open, because "when no personality embodies [an idea], no other personality may contest it" (ibid.). Although the hipster might represent to Mailer an attractive alternative to America's present direction, he has no means of obtaining power, since the collective effort of an effective rebellion is not in his nature. "All heroes are leaders," Mailer tells us (ibid.). They are capable of attaining and holding power and of representing their ideas. The channels of power being what they are, the practical solution would be to elect as president a heroic leader. And heroes are *made*, not born, in Mailer's canon; in fact they make themselves, they are existentialists. "Existential politics," Mailer tells us, "is rooted in the concept of the hero, it would argue that the hero is the one kind of man who *never* develops by accident, that a hero is a consecutive set of brave and witty self-creations" (ibid.). "The basic argument" of existential politics, he goes on, is that "if there is a strong ineradicable strain in human nature, one must not try to suppress it or anomaly, cancer, and plague will follow. Instead one must find an art into which it can grow" (*PP*, p. 35). Following his own argument, Mailer substitutes for the ineffectual hipster the existential hero who can make himself grow. The concept is a key one, not only for an understanding of *An American Dream* but also for Mailer's future artistic development. If you can't find a hero, make one, goes the theory, and if you can't make *him* into a hero, make yourself into one. Stephen Richards Rojack is Mailer's most significant attempt to create a hero other than himself.

So Rojack at the outset separates himself from the found hero, Kennedy. He records for us at the book's beginning the key experience which turned him into an existentialist. It occurred during the war on a night with a full moon. Some mysterious power, referred to as "it" or "the grace," entered Rojack and led him to kill four German machine gunners. The fourth soldier confronted him and forced Rojack to look into his eyes, containing knowledge which went "back all the way to God" (*AAD*, p. 12). Rojack faltered before the soldier's stare, and the mysterious presence deserted him because of his cowardice. Later Rojack realizes that the eyes "had come to see what was waiting on the other side and they told me then that death was a creation more dangerous than life" (p. 14). This is the glimpse of the abyss which remained with him as the authentic experience of his life, while the pattern he followed after the war, that of the conventional twentieth-century American Dream, proved false. Out of his experience he had developed his thesis that "magic, dread, and the perception of death were the roots of motivation" (*AAD*, p. 15), but he had not tested the thesis further. Instead, he became a "professor of existential psychology," attempting to teach his thesis to others while sensing that only through experiencing it could one know its authenticity. Having arrived at the conclusion that he is a failure (although he has a Ph.D., a full professorship, a popular television show, and a rich wife), Rojack gets down to basics. He wishes a more authentic self, one in line with the one meaningful experience in his life; and that self is obtainable only through an act of violence which wrenches it free of the false self and allows it to create itself anew. Suicide is the only other alternative Rojack sees, for he cannot continue with the roles he has been playing.

The strongest tie to his old life is his relationship with his wife, Deborah. Like the "bitch goddess" Leslie Fiedler has shown us to be characteristic in modern American literature,[6] Deborah has worked at psychologically castrating Rojack, but yet he is so bound to her by the ferocity of both his love and his hate that the only way to be free of her is either to take his own life or hers. He cannot escape from her to a far place as could his mythic predecessors, Rip Van Winkle or Huck Finn. Like Jay Gatsby, Rojack's creation of himself in his own image exposes the newborn self to the extreme dangers of a corrupt environment, and the unfit are either killed like Gatsby or, knowing evil, search for a new environment capable of sustaining life, as Rojack will come to do.

Rojack's narration of present events begins with an experience on a friend's balcony in which the moon, which throughout the novel lights up Rojack's perceptions of death and of the depths of his own being, reflects his suicidal desires; since his life is deadening, perhaps he should give it up before it is wholly dead and save his soul from extinction. Mailer's belief is that the soul migrates after death, unless one has killed it through a cowardly, suppressive existence. By entertaining the idea of suicide, Rojack can feel all that is noble in himself, his "courage," "wit," "ambition and hope" rising to the moon, while "a growth against the designs of [his] organs," a cancerous growth, begins in his body (*AAD*, p. 20). This is Rojack's second authentic experience. His choices have been narrowed down quite literally to life or death. The benefit of the experience is that he has been stripped of his trappings and is in touch with his deepest being. Throughout the novel from this point on Rojack hears a voice in his mind whenever he must make a vital choice. The voice is either that navigator at the seat of our being (discussed earlier) or the voice of old, deadened habit, and Rojack must learn to listen to the one and deny the other. The first represents the subconscious, instinctual life in tune with the senses. It is like the guide in a dream-vision who must be trusted in peril. Rojack's progress after this point is developed in terms of a series of tests in which he

must make the right choices with or without the aid of the
voices or pay for his mistakes. Mailer's organizing principle
and theme in this novel as in so much of his work is "grow
or pay."

The movement of *An American Dream* may be seen as a
spiral similar to that of *Advertisements for Myself*. The action of the novel, concentrated into a period of approximately thirty-two hours, or, more significantly, two nights and a
day, is exemplary of Mailer's concept of time as "the connection of new circuits," for time is used here symbolically, as
in a dream, rather than literally. It is foolish to complain, as
some reviewers have, that the novel's action could not realistically have taken place in such a short time span.

On another level, the novel as originally written was a
race against clock time, for Mailer wrote it in eight install-
ments for *Esquire* magazine.[7] Although the material was
considerably rewritten for the hardback edition, the tight
episodic structure of the novel was retained. Mailer looked
upon the serial form as a test of his imaginative and writing
powers, although he did not at the outset expect that the
book would have "the huge proportions and extreme ambition" of the big book described in *Advertisements for Myself*.[8]

Like the novel itself, then, its potential hero was to bloom
overnight. Following the balcony scene, Rojack ventures
into the late March night air. The season obviously is ripe
for a rebirth. His first action, after having described the par-
asitic nature of his relationship with Deborah—she "occup-
ie[s] [his] center" (*AAD*, p. 32)—is to telephone his wife and
to be drawn to her by the residual force he must overcome.
His senses still sharp from the balcony episode, Deborah's
apartment impresses him as a perfumed jungle, which it
proves to be. Deborah is a powerful adversary, the Devil's
child we come to learn, with all of his subtlety and strength
to overcome. Her malignity is palpable to Rojack and the inevitable battle to the death ensues. Deborah is described as
a bull, in a reversal of male and female roles, who tries to
"mangle" Rojack's "root" (*AAD*, p. 35). As he succeeds in

strangling her, he has a vision of "heaven," "some quiver of jeweled cities shining in the glow of a tropical dusk" (ibid.) like the New Jerusalem or the Renaissance vision of the New World. On an allegorical level Rojack's action is equivalent to the American Revolution, while on a mythic level he is reborn. A "new grace" infuses him, his "flesh seem[s] new" (*AAD*, p. 36). Now the newborn soul, created through the act of murdering another, must try to survive in a hostile environment. If Deborah's murder is the historical equivalent of the American Revolution, Rojack's subsequent action is conducted in the present, in the America which has become as corrupt as the old world. Brom Weber has observed that unlike most novels, in *An American Dream* "the climatic moment occurs at the beginning; the processes, concepts, and values of reason are literally and symbolically destroyed at that stage. Thereafter only the psychic growth of Rojack is consequential; his perceptions must create a world where before there was merely arid thought disguising nothingness."[9] The world to be created is the jeweled city in the fertile tropics as opposed to the neon city in the arid desert which is Hell.

The metaphoric level which Mailer develops in this novel runs parallel to the literal level, as in a medieval dream-vision, and the two levels constantly enrich one another with each detail contributing to the total pattern. If Deborah is evil and corruption, all that is associated with her is corrupt as well: the Catholic church, the family fortune imaged as "the filthy-lucred wealth of all the world" (*AAD*, p. 38), her father the Devil and the incestuous child they presumably beget. Not content, as he suspects his contemporaries are, to write a novel which is only "a paw of the beast" (*CC*, p. 99), Mailer heaps metaphor upon metaphor in an attempt at "a creation equal to the phenomenon of the country itself," the Great American Novel.

It may be argued that the novel suffers from a certain thinness because of its heavy reliance on metaphor and allegory. Ironically, many early reviewers took it quite literally and found the violence and uncommon sexual acts particularly offensive, whereas these acts express Mailer's existential ethics on the metaphorical level. Although Mailer believes that the novel has "no right to exist unless it exists on the literal level," he argues that the characters perceive and experience reality differently, more intensely and psychically, than ordinary people.[10]

The war between good and evil for possession of America is central to Mailer's vision. Remembering an earlier conversation with Deborah, Rojack emphasizes this elemental nature of the American experience. "I know that I am more good and more evil than anyone alive," Deborah tells Rojack, "but which was I born with, and what came into me? . . . I'm evil if truth be told," she goes on, "But I despise it, truly I do. It's just that evil has power." "Which is a way of saying," Rojack interprets, "goodness was imprisoned by evil." (*AAD*, p. 40). It has long been the sad theme of American literature and in turn the oldest story of man that the serpent has entered the garden. What Mailer provides for in Rojack is a confrontation with the serpent and a chance to make good as powerful as evil. Mailer's perception of God and the Devil as warring but equal visions of the universe adds dimension to Rojack's struggle. Good is not inevitably doomed as in Hawthorne or Mark Twain. Now that Rojack has attracted the attention of the gods by taking life and death into his own hands, they will act out their war through him. So Rojack's fate is that of God as well.

Rojack awakes from resting beside Deborah's body to a rainbow, like a covenant, at "the edge of [his] vision" (*AAD*, p. 41). A heightened awareness, similar to that obtained through drugs, and a feeling of grace remain with him after the murder, evidence of the rightness of his choice. Through the defeat of his worthy opponent, "what was good in her had been willed to [him]" (p. 43). He is directed by a messenger from his subconscious to engage in sex with Deborah's German maid, Ruta, whose name suggests the female complement to what he calls his "root" or sexual organ. Sex to Mailer, we may remember, is a metaphor for creation or destruction. This is precisely the choice Rojack

79

must make in his bout with Ruta: to either leave his seed in her anus, the Devil's "empty tomb," or her vagina, the Lord's "chapel." His inner voice directs him to the chapel, but on impulse he chooses the tomb. He has a "vision immediately after a huge city in the desert, in some desert, was it a place on the moon? For the colors had the unreal pastel of a plastic and the main street was flaming with light of five A.M." (*AAD*, p. 49). The city is Las Vegas, America's Hell in the desert, not the jeweled tropical city Rojack envisioned at Deborah's death. Barry H. Leeds, with whose general approach to this novel I am in accord, attributes this choice to Rojack's need of "the evil within himself in order to combat the evil besieging him in the world."[11] The implicit significance of this statement in terms of American literature is that while the American hero's typical reaction to initiation into the evils of adulthood or "civilized" society is madness, the desire to escape, or a debilitating assimilation, Mailer's hero must learn to handle evil not simply to survive but in order to become good and to create goodness around him. Leeds and others have compared Rojack's progress to a pilgrimage, and in the exemplum of a pilgrimage the pilgrim's success or failure is the possibility of the reader's own. As in the myth of the fortunate fall, goodness cannot be preserved without a knowledge of evil, and true innocence is ignorance. Rojack's experiences subsequent to his rebirth at Deborah's death test his ability not to overcome temptations but to combat evil itself, as a type of Saint George.

Under the power gained through leaguing with the Devil, Rojack returns to the scene of the crime. He restrains strong desires to mutilate and feast upon Deborah's body, like a primitive ingesting his victim's courage by eating his heart. Instead, the navigator, or "messenger" as this force is called in the novel, challenges Rojack to take the "boldest" route by throwing Deborah's body out of the tenth-story window and making her death appear a suicide (*AAD*, pp. 53–54). What is boldest about this choice lies in Rojack's combating American society's most basic function, the protection of the lives of its citizens, while undermining its enforcement of this function through a lie. Ironically, society's corruption is underscored by Rojack's choice, for normally he would have been punished for an act which society labels a crime, whereas Rojack accomplished a good by destroying Deborah's evil. Further, Rojack is later allowed to go free, because the authorities cannot be certain that he is without mighty political power.

Needing another injection of guile in order to deal with the police, Rojack returns to Ruta for a quick sexual bout. This time, however, he believes that a force within her emplants his seed in her womb, probably as payment of a life to the Devil for the life Rojack has taken from him. However, this does not prove to be adequate payment.

Rojack is now able to perform in the manner expected of him while retaining a clear mind. During interrogation, he attributes to Deborah one of Mailer's own views on the state of the soul. One may choose to commit suicide if his soul "is in danger of being extinguished," because "if the soul is extinguished in life, nothing passes on into Eternity when you die" (*AAD*, p. 68). In an essay entitled "The Metaphysics of the Belly," included in both *The Presidential Papers* and *Cannibals and Christians*, Mailer explores the relationship between the soul and the being it inhabits. A being by his definition is "anything which lives and still has the potentiality to change, to change physically and to change morally." Soul, in contrast, is "what continues to live after we are dead." It enters into a type of marriage relationship with the body it enters. Each may affect the other; they may "grow together or apart," be good or bad for each other, and the soul is "changed by its existence in the world" for better or for worse (*PP*, pp. 318–19). The concept bears obvious similarities to the Hindu's or Buddhist's karma, a word Mailer has come to use with increasing frequency.

In projecting such a view onto Deborah's action, Rojack almost comes to believe that what he says is true. His story also postulates that Deborah committed suicide because she had contracted cancer, a Mailer metaphor which, as we have seen, denotes the progressive death of the spirit. An

81

autopsy corroborates that much of Rojack's story and confirms physically Deborah's corruption.

Throughout these experiences, Rojack maintains a state of heightened awareness. His senses, particularly the olfactory, operate psychically. A passage following his interrogation illustrates the degree to which his senses resemble those of a primitive, an infant, or, in Mailer's chosen metaphor, an animal:

> Like a bird indeed in a cage in a darkened room, the passing flare of light from outside gave some memory of the forest, and I felt myself soaring out on the beating of my heart as if a climax of fear had begun which might race me through swells of excitement until everything burst, the heart burst, and I flew out to meet my death.
>   . . . I knew at last the sweet panic of an animal who is being tracked, for if danger were close, if danger came in on the breeze, and one's nostrils had an awareness of the air as close as that first touch of a tongue on your flesh, there was still such a tenderness for the hope one could stay alive. Something came out of the city like the whispering of a forest, and on the March night's message through the open window I had at that instant the first smell of spring, that quiet instant, so like the first moment of love one feels in a woman who has until then given no love. (*AAD*, pp. 74–75)

By becoming natural, that is, in touch with his own nature, Rojack is in touch with the natural world as well. Although cities have replaced forests, communication of beings to their natural environment is still possible through intense effort. The quoted passage further stresses through the two similes of sex and love the creative nature of Rojack's new being.

Temporarily free of Deborah's domination and his own fear, Rojack compares himself to a creature who "took a leap over the edge of mutation" and having "crossed a chasm of time" was now "some new breed of man" (*AAD*, p. 80). This concept of the creation of the self is very much the subject of this middle section of the novel. And like Adam, the new Rojack is incomplete without a mate. The passage in which this dawns upon him is not in the least subtle. While trying to keep his new self intact under the police interrogation and his own weakness which compelled him "to cry out that I too was insane and my best ideas were poor,

82

warped, distorted, and injurious to others," Rojack asks God for a sign, "crying it into the deeps of myself as if I possessed all the priorities of a saint." He then "looked up with conviction and desperation sufficient to command a rainbow, but there was nothing which caught my eye in the room but the long blonde hair of Cherry standing across the floor . . . the dread lifted even as I stood up and once again I felt a force in my body . . . and a voice inside me said, 'Go to the girl'" (pp. 86–88).

As her name indicates, there is something virginal and as American as cherry pie about Cherry, despite the sordidness of her past. Her Southern family background includes incest, suicide, and madness as in the Faulknerian version of the failed American dream, and her former lovers include members of the Mafia and a black musician. Cherry too is a murderer, having arranged for the removal of the boyfriend whom she believed to have been the cause of her sister's suicide. Cherry's wide experiences make her something of a representative American and therefore a candidate for spiritual renewal. While watching her nightclub act, Rojack establishes a psychic control over Cherry. He shoots an imaginary arrow into her womb and is nauseated by the sickness it releases. Like Error in the first book of *The Fairie Queene*, Rojack vomits forth all the illness within himself:

> violations, the rot and gas of compromise, the stink of old fears, mildew of discipline, all the biles of habit and the horrors of pretense. . . . I felt like some gathering wind which drew sickness from the lungs and livers of others and passed them through me and up and out into the water. . . . if the murderer were now loose in me, well, so too was a saint of sorts, a minor saint no doubt, but free at last to absorb the ills of others and regurgitate them forth, ah yes, this was communion. (*AAD*, p. 98)

A feeling of peace follows, expressed in this surprising simile: "Nausea faded like the echo of a locomotive," surely an unusual image for a contemporary American novelist but characteristic of nineteenth-century writers, as Leo Marx has shown us in *The Machine in the Garden*. The locomotive is an antipastoral symbol, the literal "machine in the garden" of America, and here Mailer removes it from *his* creation. He removes as well the condition of the Sartrean existentialist as he contemplates his terrifying freedom—nausea. Rojack's growing self-assurance results not so much from his action in the novel as from his author's vision of his eventual end, that is, of the metaphorical significance attached to his actions. The making of a viable hero to serve as an exemplum at this stage of Mailer's thinking is still the province of the novelist-creator. The voices or instincts which lead Rojack to the actions he takes emanate from the Creator of Being who is Mailer and only God by analogy.

The major test of Rojack's potential for heroism lies in the strength of his love of and loyalty to Cherry. Her kernel of virtue amid the accumulations of corruption is more assumed than demonstrated. As she is the representative American who may be saved by Rojack's heroism, she is also a metaphor for America itself and of its possible survival if its core of goodness is strong enough to combat the evil which has enclosed it.

Cherry, too, is a proponent of Mailer's suicide theory, of dying while there is something to attach one's soul to on the other side; whereas Rojack, now experienced in resisting the suicidal impulse, is characterized by Cherry as an "optimist" for his belief in the gain to one's strength in choosing to live. But Rojack still dreads death. The moon is to be full for three more days, signifying that Rojack is a type of Christ who must conquer death in that symbolic length of time. The way to life is through loving Cherry courageously.

Rojack's initiation into love is conducted amidst a carefully constructed environment. The physical surroundings are odious; Cherry's apartment is the one in which her sister committed suicide. The time, appropriately, is dawn. Rojack and Cherry begin by being truthful with each other, then start to make love, not "as lovers, more like animals in a quiet mood":

> Nothing was loving in her; no love in me; we paid our devotions in some church no larger than ourselves. . . . Fatigue had left me all but

dead—I had no brain left, no wit, no pride, no itch, no snarl, it was as if the membrane of my past had collected like a dead skin to be skimmed away. (*AAD*, pp. 120-21)

Note the Lawrencian metaphor for the American need to slough off the past. And the religious implications of the act are stronger in the passage which follows. Rojack removes Cherry's diaphragm, "that corporate rubbery obstruction I detested so much," and the decision to create more life through love is made.

I was passing through a grotto of curious lights, dark lights, like colored lanterns beneath the sea, a glimpse of that quiver of jeweled arrows, that heavenly city which had appeared as Deborah was expiring in the lock of my arm, and a voice like a child's whisper on the breeze came up so faint I could hardly hear, "Do you want her?" it asked. "Do you really want her, do you want to know something about love at last?" and I desired something I had never known before, and answered; it was as if my voice had reached to its roots; and, "Yes," I said, "of course I do, I want love," but like an urbane old gentleman, a dry tart portion of my mind added, "Indeed, and what has one to lose?" and then the voice in a small terror, "Oh, you have more to lose than you have lost already, fail at love and you lose more than you can know." "And if I do not fail?" I asked back. "Do not ask," said the voice, "choose now!" and some continent of dread speared wide in me, rising like a dragon, as if I knew the choice was real, and in a lift of terror I opened my eyes and her face was beautiful beneath me in that rainy morning, her eyes were golden with light, and she said, "Ah, honey, sure," and I said sure to the voice in me, and felt love fly in like some great winged bird, some beating of wings at my back, and felt her will dissolve into tears, and some great deep sorrow like roses drowned in the salt of the dead came flooding from her womb and washed into me like a sweet honey of balm for all the bitter sores of my soul and for the first time in my life without passing through fire of straining the stones of my will, I came up from my body rather than down from my mind, I could not stop, some shield broke in me, bliss, and the honey she had given me I could only give back, all sweets to her womb, all come in her cunt.
"Son of a bitch," I said, "so that's what it's all about." And my mouth like a worn-out soldier fell on the heart of her breast. (*AAD*, pp. 122-23)

Portions of this passage are among the most beautiful Mailer has ever written. In touch with his deepest being, Rojack is able to choose love, and grace descends upon him like a bird. The vision of the heavenly city appears, as it did at

Deborah's murder, signifying the rightness of each choice. The time to murder an old evil part of the self is followed by a time to create an extension of the new self in another human being. Rojack watches Cherry's face metamorphosize in renewing sleep, like that of Dorian Gray after death, through the various stages of evil to that of a "golden child, . . . sweet fruit, national creation" (p. 124). Here is America, whose "separate lives must come together" in sleep (ibid.).[12]

Leaving her for his appointment with Roberts, the police detective, Rojack feels fully alive. His own vitality is once again sharply contrasted to the antipastoral locomotive: "One hundred years before, some first trains had torn through the prairie and their warning had congealed the nerve. 'Beware,' said the sound. 'Freeze in your route. Behind this machine comes a century of maniacs and a heat which looks to consume the earth' " (*AAD*, p. 125). We are reminded of the nightmare which crossed the continent in the name of the American Dream. And Rojack is reminded of the pact he made with the Devil through Ruta before making one with the Lord through Cherry. Which will prove the stronger is the central question of the remainder of the novel.

Having acted with Cherry as a whole man, Rojack now, apart from her, is cognizant of his "separate parts: college professor, television performer, marginal socialite, author, police suspect, lecher, newly minted lover of a thrush named Cherry. I had roots, weed's roots: Jewish father, immigrant stock; Protestant mother, New England banking family, second-drawer" (*AAD*, p. 127). These separate roles, each requiring certain manners and behavior, however conflicting, must be shed or combined into a truer, stronger whole. The chapter begun by the vision of an authentic self through love continues with the sloughing off of old, inauthentic selves in "A Catenary of Manners," the chapter's title. Telephone calls from the producer of Rojack's television show, the chairman of his department at the university, and a socialite friend of Deborah's enable him to shed the first three roles he mentions in the quoted passage. Interestingly, por-

An American Dream

tions of some of Mailer's theories are attributed to these persons, as might happen in a dream. The producer quotes Mailer's favorite Marxian maxim, that "Quantity changes quality;" the chairman's wife believes that "the last meal a person eats before they die determines the migration of their soul" (p. 138); and the socialite is psychic with odors. From the latter Rojack also learns that Ruta is Barney Kelly's mistress and that both she and Deborah were spies and possibly double agents. This information is corroborated when Rojack is allowed to drop the role of police suspect because too much secret information might be revealed if he were prosecuted. This situation is reminiscent of that in *Barbary Shore* (and of Orwellian double think), as Rojack sees that the "secret of sanity" is "the ability to hold the maximum of impossible combinations in one's mind" (p. 150). Rojack is further reminded of a lecture he had once delivered which strikes him with "the force of a real idea."

> In contrast to the civilized view which elevates man above the animals, the primitive had an instinctive belief that he was subservient to the primal pact between the beasts of the jungle and the beast of mystery.
> To the savage, dread was the natural result of any invasion of the supernatural: if man wished to steal the secrets of the gods, it was only to be supposed that the gods would defend themselves and destroy whichever man came too close. By this logic, civilization is the successful if imperfect theft of some cluster of these secrets, and the price we have paid is to accelerate our private sense of some enormous if not quite definable disaster which awaits us. (Ibid.)

Rojack, a type of Prometheus waiting to be bound, is now surprisingly released, and his sense of dread at the unknowable reasons for the decision is greatly increased. Having gained the attention of the gods through the theft of their power to give or deny life, Rojack is brought close to nausea by the mysterious nature of the power which could control his destiny. His impending appointment at midnight with Barney Oswald Kelly is to be a confrontation with a visible portion of that mystery.

> I had a sudden hatred of mystery, a moment when I wanted to be in a cell, my life burned down to the bare lines of a legal defense. I did

> not want to see Barney Oswald Kelly later tonight, and yet I knew I must for that was part of the contract I had made on the morning air. I would not be permitted to flee the mystery. I was close to prayer then, I was very close, for what was prayer but a beseechment *not* to pursue the mystery, "God," I wanted to pray, "let me love that girl, and become a father, and try to be a good man, and do some decent work. Yes, God," I was close to begging, "do not make me go back again to the charnel house of the moon." But like a soldier on six-hour leave to a canteen, I knew I would have to return. (p. 153)

Allan J. Wagenheim and others have misinterpreted this passage to conclude that Mailer says here that marrying, becoming a father, and writing take courage enough without following where the imperatives of the self lead.[13] However much courage such a life takes, it is not the way of the hero, the hero needed by the nation or by the embattled vision of God, and should Rojack choose it he would fail to grow into that hero.

Returning to Cherry, her "gift" of "new life" returns to him:

> those wings were in the room, clear and delicate as a noble intent, that sweet presence spoke of the meaning of life for those who had betrayed it, yes I understood the meaning and said, for I knew it now, "I think we have to be good," by which I meant we would have to be brave. (*AAD*, pp. 154-55)

By making a pact with the Devil, Rojack has betrayed beforehand this love. His only hope for its survival is to commit himself totally to the good, hoping to defeat the evil and invalidate the pact. Such action requires tremendous courage and the understanding that "love was not a gift but a vow. Only the brave could live with it for more than a little while" (p. 156).

Cherry and Rojack first test the strength of their love for each other by revealing their past sins. Rojack confesses that he murdered Deborah, and Cherry that Barney Kelly had been her lover. This latter confession brings on a repetition of Rojack's vision of the city in the desert, first present when he compacted with the Devil for the cunning to get away with murder. For the moment the relationship of Kelly to Cherry, the feeling that "Kelly and I were running in the same blood," reawakens the desire to murder. But the knowledge that their love is distinguishable from "the art of the Devil" calms him (p. 166). He learns further that Cherry believes that he has impregnated her and that she had aborted earlier pregnancies by Kelly and Shago Martin. The importance to Rojack of the carrying on of his seed should be underscored by the passage quoted earlier from *Advertisements for Myself* in which Mailer defines "seed" as "the end of the potentialities seen for oneself, and every organism creates its seed out of the experience of its past and its unspoken vision or curse upon the future (p. 310)." As for Cherry, she has had her first orgasm through normal intercourse, repeating the situation in "The Time of Her Time," and it proves to be an apocalyptic orgasm for her, for she has long believed that her death would shortly follow its occurrence.

There are two major encounters remaining in the novel, both of them with Cherry's former lovers who had planted seeds of an accursed future in her womb. The weaker of the two opponents is immediately confronted. Shago Martin, a kind of hipster turned beat, appears at Cherry's apartment. He is the Negro mythologized in "The White Negro," complete with the coolness of the jazz musician. As in a dream where all the characters have a tight circle of relationships, Shago has not only been Cherry's lover but also has met Deborah and replaced Rojack's television show with his own. As a "captive of white shit," Shago's color is the reverse of his true nature. Cherry accuses him of losing his black and becoming evil in a Poe-like inversion where black equals good and white evil.[14]

The inevitable fight that ensues between Shago and Rojack and its sexual and power implications have been well analyzed by Leeds. The outcome of the fight is most important here. Shago has been badly beaten, and Rojack is sickened by the knowledge that he has gone too far: "It had all gone wrong again. I could feel the break in the heavens" (*AAD*, p. 184). For Shago still retained much of his goodness, and Cherry had once loved him as she now loved Rojack, but neither she nor Shago had proved brave enough to keep it alive. Cherry's belief that "God is weaker because I didn't turn out well" is of course Mailer's and central to this novel. As in a Socratic dialogue, Rojack asks a leading question, "You don't believe everything is known before it happens?"

"Oh, no," Cherry replies. "Then there's no decent explanation for evil. I believe God is just doing *His* best to learn from what happens to some of us. Sometimes, I think He knows less than the Devil because we're not good enough to reach Him. So the Devil gets most of the best messages we think we're sending up." (p. 185)

Cherry adds that these ideas first came to her in Las Vegas, the city in the desert in Rojack's vision where Mailer himself began thinking about writing *An American Dream*.[15]

Rojack has second thoughts concerning his ability to ascend the mountain of love,[16] for not only is he too quick to betray Cherry, but also he intuits that years in the future she will become a bitch. Although Cherry passes on to him Shago's umbrella, symbol of his manhood and power, Rojack instinctively feels that she is not safe from harm by Shago. Nevertheless, ignoring his instincts, he leaves her, a mistake which is to be compounded into disastrous proportions later. Mailer here prepares us for the novel's outcome. Two voices now vie for control in Rojack's mind: one tells him to go to Harlem and assure Cherry's safety; the other to go to Kelly. He cannot choose between them. He knows that he should do what he fears most, perform the bravest act, for that would have the largest gain; he knows that he should "trust the authority of [his] senses" (*AAD*, p. 191), but his fear is so great that he loses touch with them. Instead he allows the taxi in which he is riding to carry him to Kelly. Believing that "God was not love but courage" and that "love came only as a reward," Rojack is nevertheless overcome with fear:

I no longer had the confidence my thoughts were secret to myself. No, men were afraid of murder, but not from a terror of justice so much as the knowledge that a killer attracted the attention of the gods; then your mind was not your own, your anxiety ceased to be neurotic, your dread was real. Omens were as tangible as bread. There was an architecture to eternity which housed us as we dreamed, and when there was murder, a cry went through the market places of sleep. Eternity had been deprived of a room. Somewhere the divine rage met a fury. (Pp. 191–192)

The fury, or agent of demonic wrath, is Barney Oswald Kelly. Rojack's meeting with Kelly is the novel's climax. Kelly has been portrayed as the Devil with a face. His rooms at the top of the Waldorf Towers signify the power he has attained in both the natural and supernatural worlds. He is a corrupt Horatio Alger who has ruthlessly and cleverly worked his way from poverty to incalculable wealth and power. As Kaufmann has amply demonstrated, "America has made Kelly into a corrupt version of the Renaissance man."[17]

Rojack's midnight meeting with Kelly has all the tensions of Faust's final meeting with Mephistopheles. This is the most weighty "grow or pay" situation yet devised by Mailer. We are aware that only the most extreme courage on Rojack's part will enable him to renounce the Devil and strengthen his vow to the Lord. The title of the chapter, "At the Lion and the Serpent," signifies that the courage of the lion will be pitted against the wiliness of the serpent. The chapter is also the most thinly allegorical in the novel.

Beginning his ordeal, Rojack starts to climb the steps to the tower. Several have noted this *ascension* into Hell,[18] but not its implications: that Hell resides at the top of the power structure, as in the nightmare version of the American Dream, and that, further, the ascension, if successfully completed, can lead to transcendence of the nightmare. The climb precipitates a vision of Hell in America. Central to this vision is "a nineteenth-century clock, eight feet high with a bas relief of faces: Franklin, Jackson, Lincoln, Cleveland, Washington, Grant, Harrison, and Victoria; 1888 the year: in a ring around the clock was a bed of tulips which looked so like plastic I bent to touch and discovered they were real" (*AAD*, p. 194). The year 1888 marks the end of the frontier and the beginning of the machine age, thanks to the efforts of the heroic figures whose concepts of the American Dream were turned to nightmares by the machine, as the real flowers were confused with machine-made imitations. Rojack knows that the heroic action called for now would be to climb the stairs representing the various stages leading to the tower, symbol of the apocalyptic meeting which is to take place. But yet he takes the elevator or "cage" instead. As it ascends he feels that "some certainty of love was passing away, some knowledge it was the reward for which to live" (p. 196). Denying the voice that urges him to go to Harlem to save Cherry, he is denying the saving grace of that love; and although his decision to confront Kelly may have been the wiser, our expectations that Rojack will prove heroic are diminishing.

On reaching Kelly's quarters, the door to which bears his coat of arms with the motto "Victoria in Caelo Terraque," Rojack must prepare to meet the Devil in stages, through several of his servants. Ruta's presence revitalizes his demonic powers, while his visit with Deidre, Deborah's daughter, brings him comfort. Deidre is one of Mailer's ephemeral children with wisdom beyond her years. Through her we obtain our first hint that she is a product of an incestuous relationship between Deborah and Kelly, like Death born of Sin and Satan in *Paradise Lost*. Deidre recalls an incident in which she was provoked to call her mother a beast, to which Deborah replied, "Beware of beasts. There's a species which stays alive three days after they die" (p. 200). The caveat is, of course, directed at Rojack, and the implication that Deborah is a type of anti-Christ is strengthened.

Armed with this warning, Rojack is ushered into Kelly's presence. He is in the company of two of his earthly lieutenants, Bess, his first lover, now an old woman reputed to be "the most evil woman ever to live on the Riviera," and Eddie Ganucci, a mobster king. To Rojack's psychic nose, the odors Kelly gives off make his presence "more real to [him] as an embodiment of Deborah than of himself" (p. 204). The beast in Deborah now inhabits Kelly's body until the time that it may lodge itself in another, and Rojack is clearly its object. Rojack's intuitive fear that the evil soul may take possession of him leads him to reinact the scene near the novel's beginning, in which he contemplates suicide by jumping off a balcony in order to save his soul. He has "a sudden thought":

> "If you loved Cherry, you would jump," which was an abbreviation for the longer thought that there was a child in her, and death, my death, my violent death, would give some better heart so that embryo just created, that indeed I might even be created again, free of my past. (P. 210)

But as we have learned from earlier works of Mailer's, freedom from the past is obtained only by coming to terms with it, and one must make such an effort before one may truly create a desirable future. This is what Rojack must now do. He must face Barney Kelly, who on all levels—as his murdered wife's father, as the American power structure given a face, as a corrupt Renaissance and Adamic figure, as Rojack's mythic father, and as the personification of Satan—must be defeated or Rojack can neither move forward, grow out of his past into the future, nor become a hero without waging psychic war against all that Kelly represents. "God exists," he thinks, as "a vast calm altogether aware of me" (ibid.), and we are prepared for an apocalyptic moment in which the lieutenant of God meets the agent of the Devil more nakedly than we are ever again to see in Mailer's work. Whether Mailer can write Rojack out of this situation depends upon his vision of the future.

A voice tells Rojack to walk the parapet outside Kelly's apartment.[19] It is a test of his will over his dread. His will remains "divided against itself" (*AAD*, p. 211), but his intuition of God arms him for the encounter with Kelly. It is made in Kelly's library, painstakingly detailed as a decadent Renaissance nightmare. Rojack progressively feels it as a "royal chapel," "the interior of a cave," and "an antechamber of Hell" where "a field of force" comes upon him (pp. 219-20). He still carries Shago's umbrella which brings him temporary strength, like a shield, as Kelly begins a discussion of God and the Devil. As one of Satan's agents, he reveals that the Catholic Church and organized power "from the Muslims to the *New York Times*" all work in the Devil's behalf. He goes on to account for his rise to power from impoverished beginnings. The story is, of course, that of the American Dream transmogrified. Kelly marries wealth, *European* wealth, to complete the picture of corruption, and, conceiving Deborah in the name of Satan, his luck turns into infallible power. "There's nothing but magic at the top," Kelly confides, because "God and the Devil are very attentive to the people at the summit." One must "be ready to deal with One or the Other" or settle for mediocrity (p. 230). We are reminded of Rojack's prayer to be allowed to become a family man.

As was the case in the significant meetings between Cherry and Rojack, he and Kelly now expose their secrets to each other, thus meeting as equals. Kelly reveals his incestuous relationship with Deborah, and Rojack counters with a confession of murder. The nakedness of their confrontation as agents of God and the Devil imparts a strong psychic dimension. Rojack feels as a force Kelly's invitation to a *menage à trois* with Ruta, to "bury the ghost of Deborah by gorging on her corpse" (p. 237). This is followed by another vision, that Shago is with Cherry or that someone is being murdered in Harlem, and again Rojack is so overcome with dread that he prays "to be free of magic, the tongue of the Devil, the dread of the Lord" (p. 238). But instead the messenger within him tells him to "walk the parapet or Cherry is dead," to walk it or he himself is "worse than dead" (ibid.).

The parapet walk is now the ultimate existential battle, with life and death, the victory of God or the Devil in America as its outcome. Relinquishing Shago's umbrella to Kelly, Rojack steps up onto the parapet. The language in this passage is highly metaphorical, as charged with tension as a high-voltage wire. The parapet is three sided. Making the first turn (equivalent to murdering Deborah), Rojack sees the street below: "the fall seemed twice as far, and then opened again like a crack in the earth, which deepened as I looked into it and fell away and opened out again bottom-less" (p. 241). It is the abyss, of course, which Rojack has glimpsed. Halfway into the second segment a storm arises and Deborah's "lone green eye" clouds his vision. Again two conflicting voices give orders. His cowardice tells him to get off while he can and his courage instructs him to look at the moon. The moon sends this message: "You murdered. So you are in her cage. Now, earn your release. Go around the parapet again" (p. 242). Gaining confidence, Rojack completes the first circuit, but as he is to begin the second passage, so clearly crucial to his salvation, Kelly tries to push him off with Shago's umbrella. Rojack manages to strike Kelly with the umbrella, then hurls it over the parapet, but his courage goes with it. Ignoring the voice telling him to walk the parapet again, he takes the "cage" to the street. Dread and a sense of woe invade him, for he knows that he has failed, and that the love that is a reward for courage will be denied him. He arrives at Cherry's apartment in time to watch her die from a beating mistakenly imposed by a friend of Shago's. Shago, too, has perished in a Harlem fight. Deborah's life is paid for with Cherry's life because of Rojack's weakness. In the course of the novel's action Rojack has proved his thesis that "magic, dread, and the perception of death [are] the roots of motivation,"[20] and that love was not a strong enough motive in the final analysis.

The epilogue to *An American Dream* centers on the role that America has played in Rojack's defeat. Engaged in a search for new life and for the heroism mature enough to combat demonic force, Rojack heads West, the archetypal direction toward renewal in American history and literature. The body of America is imaged as cancerous, horribly decayed. Its odor is ever present in Las Vegas, the city of fire and ice in the desert which is Hell. The extreme heat of the desert countered by the cold of air-conditioned buildings is metaphorically equivalent to the two rivers of rationality and madness which America has not succeeded in combining. The West once so promising is now cancer producing.

The atmosphere is that of an air-conditioned nightmare, to borrow Henry Miller's metaphor, as Mailer has, and the "arid empty wild blind deserts" of the West are "producing again a new breed of man," (*AAD*, p. 251) one more suited to a submarine or a space capsule than to his natural habitat. Mailer is to pick up this theme more strongly fifteen years later in *Of A Fire on the Moon*. For now, Rojack gambles the remnant of Cherry's gift to him, makes a small fortune, and prepares to leave America. Metaphorically, the message here is that America's remaining opportunity is the good fortune to be able to leave her.

Just before leaving Las Vegas, Rojack walks into the desert to look at the moon:

> There was a jeweled city on the horizon, spires rising in the night, but the jewels were diadems of electric and the spires were the neon of signs ten stories high. *I was not good enough to climb up and pull them down.* So wandered out to the desert where the mad before me had come and thought of walking into ambush. . . . I was safe in the city—no harm would come to me there—it was only in the desert that death would come up like a scorpion with its sting. (*AAD*, pp. 251-52, italics mine)

Rojack's vision of the jeweled city of heaven in a fertile jungle which appeared like a promise at Deborah's death is not to be found in its inversion, this artificial city in the wasteland of Hell. His final vision is of Cherry in the limbo of the moon, along with her archetype, Marilyn Monroe. Dying before their souls were dead, they have escaped the fate in store for America.

Leaving the nightmarish wasteland behind him, Rojack heads south to the symbolic jungles of Guatemala and Yucatan, carrying with him not only the possibility of his own salvation but the hope of a new America in Central America as well. Like Natty Bumppo and Huck Finn, Rojack lights out for the territory untouched by "civilization," but unlike his fictional predecessors, Rojack does not wish to escape so much as to continue "to grow on the waves of the violent, the perfumed, and the unexpected." The forces of evil have proved too powerful for his weak, embryonic heroism. Perhaps the new territory will provide the nourishment America lacks and so enable Rojack to grow to maturity. Perhaps he will yet develop the strength to effectively combat the Devil. In this light, Rojack's American Dream has been successful. Having come to terms with his past, having learned something about "the beast of mystery," he can move out into the future and truly remake himself not out of weakness but of strength.

At this point in time, Mailer could not visualize a hero capable of recreating America within its present boundaries. He must begin anew in a new place. This option is open to the visionary and the writer of fiction, but not to the man living in and with the "real" world. In *An American Dream* Mailer has given us a great imaginative vision of America, one which surely will secure him a place among those American writers who have told us the most about ourselves. Nevertheless, he feels a strong responsibility to remake the America he sees about him. His fictional hero inadequate to the task, Mailer himself will try to become the man of our time. His progress toward that goal is the subject of the following chapter.

NOTES

1. *Time*, March 30, 1962, p. 84.
2. Norman Mailer. "Introduction," in *Deaths for the Ladies (and other disasters)*, no pagination.
3. John William Corrington, "An American Dreamer," p. 66.
4. Northrop Frye, *Anatomy of Criticism*, pp. 33–34.
5. Norman Mailer, *An American Dream*, p. 15. All further references are cited in the text, and the title will be abbreviated to *AAD.*
6. Leslie Fiedler, *Love and Death in the American Novel*, p. 329 et passim.
7. The novel appeared from January to August 1964 in *Esquire* and as a book in 1965.
8. Norman Mailer, "The Big Bite," p. 26.
9. Brom Weber, "A Fear of Dying," p. 6.
10. Laura Adams, "Existential Aesthetics: An Interview with Norman Mailer," p. 199.
11. *The Structured Vision of Norman Mailer*, p. 126.
12. Mailer has admitted (see the interview cited above) that Cherry is not an altogether successful character, because she is not fully developed. She is successful as a metaphor, however.

13. Allan J. Wagenheim, "Square's Progress," p. 68.
14. Cf. Poe's *The Narrative of Arthur Gordon Pym.*
15. Mailer, "The Big Bite," p. 26.
16. Mailer's use of the mountain metaphor will be remembered from *The Naked and the Dead.*
17. Donald Kaufmann, *Norman Mailer: The Countdown/The First Twenty Years,* pp. 77–78.
18. Wagenheim, "Square's Progress," p. 54, among others.
19. For an interesting analysis of the parapet as a metaphor in Mailer's work see Tony Tanner, *City of Words,* pp. 348–71 (reprinted in Laura Adams, ed., *Will the Real Norman Mailer Please Stand Up?*).
20. For an account of magic as Rojack's mode of perception see Stanley T. Gutman, "*An American Dream*: New Modes of Perception" in "Mankind in Barbary," pp. 137–79.

3

PHASE THREE: *THE ARMIES OF THE NIGHT*

The Process

The years following the publication of the final version of *An American Dream* find Mailer expanding in all directions, using both media new to him and existing literary genres in new ways. In slightly more than two years Mailer authored a collection of essays, a Broadway play, two films (which he also starred in and directed), a photographic interpretation of bullfighting, a novel, numerous magazine articles, and finally a book entitled *The Armies of the Night: The Novel as History/History as a Novel.* The form developed in *Armies* was the product of Mailer's determined search for a style and a hero appropriate to that style during these years of 1966 through the spring of 1968. That Mailer found the style and vision of *Armies* a felicitous marriage is evidenced by the bulk of the work which has followed, seven books in basically the same mode.[1]

A chronological approach to Mailer's work in the years between *An American Dream* and *The Armies of the Night* will enable us to see the ways in which *Armies* is the culmination of a phase in Mailer's career and in some sense also of twenty years of living and writing.

In 1966 Mailer was a witness for the defense at the Boston trial of *Naked Lunch* on obscenity charges. He was deeply impressed by Burroughs's work, to which an essay written in 1963, "Some Children of the Goddess," will attest. Mailer saw Burroughs's vision of the future in *Naked Lunch* as that of an "all-electronic universe" described in language that "bombard[s]" the reader like the "maximum disturbance" of technological noise (*CC*, pp. 116–17). The highly charged relentlessness of Burroughs's style is also impressive to Mailer, although he places little emphasis on Burroughs's subject in *Naked Lunch*, the nature of addiction, seemingly a subject which would interest him. Rereading the book three years later while its contents were on trial, Mailer was engaged in analyzing its art and concluding that a style which forced the reader into new modes of perception, as Burroughs's did, was the only style worthy of emulation. It was at about this period that Mailer's last published novel, *Why Are We in Vietnam?*, was conceived, and it will be argued later that the style of that novel derived in part from Mailer's encounter with *Naked Lunch*, particularly the technique of bombarding the reader with language. The principle behind this technique is that of nullifying conventional language with the force of one's own, thereby breaking the language barrier by requiring a new consciousness of the reader. The recognition of this technique in the early part of the period now under discussion marks a turning point in Mailer's thinking. Convinced that the mass media which rely on technological means of communication, especially the news media, the Hollywood film, and television, abuse their intent to communicate "truth" or "reality," Mailer attempts to provide an alternative to their deadening effects. He seeks authentic uses for these media, ways of communicating through technology how technology tends to destroy creativity, thought, and spontaneity, turning its viewers and readers into extensions of itself. It is as if Mailer at this point began to suspect that the novel, the poem, the story—the conventional literary genres to which he had devoted so much of his talent and energy—were no longer capable of influencing the masses, and that the revolution in the consciousness of our time would have to be abandoned or approached through radically different means. Much of the work that he produced in these years is experimentation with technological or semitechnological means of reaching an audience. Mailer's experiments with synthesizing technology and art represent a major step forward in his thinking, for heretofore his approach to the machine had been solely antithetical: destroy it in order to recreate humanity, while a synthesis of art and technology allows the artist to control and therefore transcend the machine, bringing about expansion, growth, and new theses and antitheses.

During this phase Mailer's search for new ways of reaching an audience resulted in few works that would be considered to have lasting value. As parts of the continuing process of Mailer's growth, however, each work has a unique value. And two of these, *Why Are We in Vietnam?* and *The Armies of the Night*, are outstanding efforts by Mailer to communicate his ideas about America. Well conceived both thematically and aesthetically, they represent significant advances over *An American Dream* most especially in the conception of the author-audience relationship. On first reading, the content of *An American Dream* alienates the majority of its audience, even the presumably sophisticated, as a survey of the novel's reviews will reveal. Similarly, *Vietnam* tends to alienate through style and language, although its message probably is repugnant to fewer readers, evidenced by the growing portion of the American populace that opposed the war in Vietnam. This is not to say that these novels have no artistic unity; they do. However, I am convinced that the separation of form and content is less difficult for casual readers than for students of literature, and that as a consequence few readers of either book comprehended the medium or the message. For Mailer this failure to connect with his audience is more than a blow to his ego; it largely negates the work itself, for its intention is to influence, to affect change, to become a part of an expanding human consciousness. *The Armies of the Night*, which fuses form and content through the participation of a believable hero in an actual event, illustrates that Mailer has learned how to capture the audience he needs to fulfill his goal. The fact that the book received the nation's two highest literary awards, the National Book Award and the Pulitzer Prize, supports this contention. For these reasons I consider *The Armies of the Night* Mailer's most mature work to date in terms of his own philosophical and artistic goals, although it is likely that instructors in American literature will favor the last two novels because they fit so well into the continuum of American literature as taught in universities.

Another phase of the process which culminated in *The Armies of the Night* began in 1966. While Mailer was ingesting the electronic style of William Burroughs, he was publishing another of his thematically unified collections of odds and ends, *Cannibals and Christians*. If Mailer's personality had served as the substantial armature of *Advertisements for Myself*, his reputation and his constant theme of the sixties, that America is "Cancer Gulch," hold *Cannibals and Christians* together. The book consists largely of political essays written since 1964 or literary efforts—criticism, poems, and stories—written prior to 1964. Mailer organized the varied collection on the basis that all the pieces are "parts of a continuing and more or less comprehensive vision of existence" á la Lawrence, Miller, and Hemingway (*CC*, p. xi). One considers this a given proposition, and perhaps *Cannibals and Christians* needs no further justification. Robert Lawler, a perceptive critic of Mailer's writing, sees further unity in the volume's junction of the political with the literary: "Politics, the obscene and the craft of fiction necessarily form a cohesive whole in Mailer's mind, for politics *is* the obscene of his times, as he sees it, and the writer must face both (and be involved in both) and deal with them if he is to be more than a symptom of the disease."[2]

102

The Armies of the Night

In *Cannibals and Christians*, Mailer selects the metaphorical role of physician to a society dying of the plague, his goal something akin to spontaneous remission of the disease by inspiring each of us to free ourselves of the plague. Rojack had been as successful a patient as he could conceive of given the state of society; Mailer now tries to promote the cure on a larger scale. He is still convinced, however, that the most effective treatment is through the pages of a novel. Already the doctor is prescribing a purgative, a central metaphor in *Why Are We in Vietnam?*. Looking forward to that book we may focus attention on two key elements in *Cannibals and Christians*: Vietnam as the metaphoric American Armageddon and explorations into the nature of form.

The question which has obsessed and continues to obsess Mailer through all of his succeeding works is raised again and again in these essays: Is America "extraordinary or accursed" (*CC*, p. 42)? Mailer operates on the assumption that if accursed, America can still battle to be extraordinary, and that if extraordinary, she is perilously close to accursedness. While here he seems to equate the extraordinary with good and the accursed with evil, there remains the third possibility that the extraordinary attracts accursedness by attracting the attention of the gods. In a memorable piece on the Republican Convention of 1964 Mailer uses the suicides of his prototypical romantic heroes, Hemingway and Marilyn Monroe, and the assassination of John Kennedy to evidence the madness turned inward, the cannibalism of a nation feeding upon its vitals which is a sure symptom of its death throes. Whether America's imminent demise is for the overall good or ill in the universal battle for possession of the universe is the great ambiguity for Mailer. However, rather than take the philosophical route of the eighteenth century, that whatever is is right, Mailer conducts his own battle for America's survival. With the deaths of his candidates for heroism and with the expatriation of his fictional hero, Rojack, Mailer in these years is coming to rely more heavily upon his own potential heroism. He becomes more active politically, centering attention on the war in Vietnam and on Lyndon Johnson as the faces of insanity in American life:

> The great fear that lies upon America is not that Lyndon Johnson is privately close to insanity so much as that he is the expression of the near insanity of most of us, and his need for action is America's need for action; not brave action, but action; any kind of action; any move to get the motors going. A future death of the spirit lies close and heavy upon American life, a cancerous emptiness at the center which calls for a circus. (*CC*, pp. 77–78)

Mailer sees something bestial in the idea of the "Great Society," "the most advanced technological nation of the civilized world," as "the one now closest to blood, to shedding the blood and burning the flesh of Asian peasants it had never seen" (*CC*, p. 79). The rhetoric here suggests that of an inflammatory speech, which it is, Mailer's "Speech at Berkeley on Vietnam Day" in 1965, a precedent for his appearance in the 1967 march on the Pentagon.

A third quotation will complete Mailer's theory on the purgative nature of the Vietnamese War:

> . . . the only explanation I can find for the war in Vietnam is that we are sinking into the swamps of a plague and the massacre of strange people seems to relieve this plague. If one were to take the patients in a hospital, give them guns and let them shoot on pedestrians down from hospital windows you may be sure you would find a few miraculous cures. (*CC*, p. 91)

Vietnam, then, to Mailer represents an outlet for violence which would otherwise be directed against the self. It is cowardly action, however, no better than suicide, for no matter how Johnson and his advisors may justify it, the war consists of violence for its own sake. This is the case because the opposition is no match for the aggressor. Remember that for Mailer, as for Hemingway and Faulkner, the worthy defeat of a worthy opponent is a brave action, and the victor gains the courage of his defeated opponent as his prize. However, the defeat of a weak opponent is cowardly brutality and propagates more cowardice and finally madness. These themes are fully developed in *Why Are We in Vietnam?*, while Mailer establishes his metaphor of Vietnam as America's Armageddon in *Cannibals and Christians*.

His thought having found its direction, even its obsession one might say—for the war and the president provided Mailer with the opposition needed to test his own potential for the role of American hero—Mailer turns his attention to his style of attack, which in turn leads him to inquiries into the nature of form itself. In an interview included in *Cannibals and Christians*, Mailer talks about keeping his consciousness in shape by "fight[ing] against diminishing talent" and by not "relax[ing] into the flabby styles of thought which surround one everywhere." Interestingly, he goes on to say that

> if what you write is a reflection of your own consciousness, then even journalism can become interesting. One wouldn't want to spend one's life at it and I wouldn't want ever to be caught justifying journalism as a major activity (it's obviously less interesting than to write a novel), but it's better, I think, to see journalism as a venture of one's ability to keep in shape than to see it as an essential betrayal of the chalice of your literary art. (Pp. 218–19)

He later conceded to journalism—albeit a highly personalized style of journalism which claims no objective truths—a force through sheer numbers of readers that the novel could no longer have, although he would bristle when Robert Lowell complimented him for being "the best journalist in America."[3] Like Hemingway, Mailer has produced more journalistic essays than fiction, although he considered it at this point as working out for the big fight.

Concerned with finding a personal style for his attack on a concrete enemy, Mailer philosophizes on the nature of form in two lengthy dialectical "interviews" with himself: "The Metaphysics of the Belly," included in both *The Presidential Papers* and *Cannibals and Christians*, and "The Political Economy of Time" in *Cannibals and Christians*. Although the latter piece contains many of the ideas that Mailer has expressed better in his fiction, it defines and clarifies certain concepts which have a way of being cryptic in the fiction. For example, here he conceives of time as "the continuation from life to death" and equates the soul with time (*CC*, p. 326). The "only container" of time is "an enlifement, that mode or character or style by which time is perceived in each different kind of being" and is thus "a set of separate creations" (p. 327). The soul, which is seen in terms of time, attaches itself to a body. There its nourishment comes from "growth and victory, from exploration, from conquest, from pomp and pageant and triumph, from glory. . . . Its nature is to become more than it is" (p. 341). The soul will try to "shape creation in its fashion" in the body it inhabits (p. 353), but if the soul is frustrated in its attempts it may be defeated and eventually die or turn into spirit. Spirits are "habits, not innovations; functions, not creations; waves, not forms; not so much the act as the context; never the event, but the institution" (p. 360). If "vision is the mind of God; soul, His Body," then "Spirit is what He left behind. Literally. It is his excrement" (p. 365). In Mailer's metaphysics the growth of one's soul is not merely a personal matter, for if the soul is allowed to die or is forcibly defeated, death and eternity no longer promise peace but may continue "the worst terrors of life" (p. 363). The growth of the soul in Mailer's mind is therefore akin to the survival of the creative power itself, of mankind's ability to perpetuate itself. As soul is time's "enlifement,"

> form is the deepest clue we possess to the nature of time in any epoch, to the style of the time, to the mode by which reality is perceived in the time to the way time moves in the consciousness of man, where it possesses grace, where it is hobbled, how strength addresses itself to weakness. Time is all but equal to creativity, for time is the potential to create as it resides in each of us. (Pp. 367-68)

In such a view time is capable of being destroyed along with creativity. We are able to evaluate the state of time and soul in any age by the form it takes, for

> form is the record of every intent of a soul to express itself upon another soul or spirit, its desire to reveal the shape—which is to say the *mystery* of the time it contains in itself. And it is aided or resisted in achieving that shape by every spirit it encounters. (P. 373)

"The Political Economy of Time" gives us perhaps the ultimate meaning of the "grow or pay" theme in Mailer's work and of the importance he attaches to victory over forces which would impede growth. At the same time we are impressed again with the concept of form as a record of growth and of the significance of the forms we discern in Mailer's work, the spiral movement of *Advertisements for Myself,* for instance. Mailer's forms are dynamic, often jagged like the charting of a corporation's profit and loss, but always moving toward something and away from something else. The more Mailer comes to rely upon an existential hero, the more the form of his fiction may be seen in terms of a line or a graph, for the hero's progress becomes measurable through confrontations won or lost. What "The Political Economy of Time" states about form, *An American Dream* in particular dramatizes and embodies.

Like the search of the soul to "shape creation in its fashion," Mailer experiments with forms and styles during 1967 which work toward media breakthroughs—new and hopefully more successful ways of reaching an audience. In *An American Dream,* it will be remembered, the hero's opponent was a personified force. In transferring Barney Kelly's role to Lyndon Johnson, Mailer points up the political face of power whose mechanics are not nearly so mysterious as Kelly's diabolics and therefore may be opposed with some expectations of success. By learning to use the communications media for his own ends rather than those of the established power structure, Mailer significantly multiplies his import.

The first media breakthrough comes early in 1967 with the Broadway production of *The Deer Park.* Terming his play "existential," Mailer sought to "occup[y] a space which had been left uninhabited too long, that area between the explorations of the realistic play and that electric sense of transition which lives in the interruptions and symbols of the Theatre of the Absurd."[4] His play was to move "from one moment of intensity or reality (which is to say a moment which feels more real than other moments) to the next—a play which went at full throttle all the way" (*DPP,*

107

p. 11). Mailer had worked for ten years on the play version of his novel, rewriting it four times before arriving at what he considered a suitable form. In the final version he "cut away all dramatic scaffolding, connective tissue, road signs, guides, and left the play stripped to its essential connections, the movement ideally from one real scene to the next, with the audience left to fill the spaces between" (ibid.). One of the more startling aspects of the play and its technological innovation is the presence of a large neon sign which flashes numbers counting down the ninety-nine scenes, the intention of which is probably to illustrate that life consists of a series of existential moments in which all significant growth or decay takes place.

The Deer Park is to be staged so that "the set bears some relation to the inner space of Sergius O'Shaugnessy's memory, that the audience is in effect living in his mind" (*DPP*, p. 33). The audience, obviously, is intended to participate in the drama, connecting the circuits left unconnected for this purpose.

Whether the play succeeded in its intended effects cannot be determined from the written version. In his dissertation on Mailer, John Stark analyzes the play as a written product and concludes that it is a "basically unsuccessful search for a new form."[5] Gerald Weales, who saw and reviewed the play during its short run of 127 performances wrote of it two years later that without the " 'dramatic scaffolding, connective tissue,' . . . an audience comes to the scenes lacking the emotional freight that the characters presumably carry, and although they will not find it difficult 'to fill the spaces' (there is exposition enough), the scenes are likely to remain dull and flat."[6] Diagnosing the play, Marshall McLuhan might have concluded that while Mailer wishes his medium to be "cool," that is, to provoke the audience to "fill the spaces" with their own sensual impressions, the play came across as an unhappy mixture of the hot and the cool, the visual effect of the flashing numbers perhaps having broken what connections the audience could make. One considers, too, the possibility that Mailer's play might have affected more strongly a less literate audience than professional Broadway play-goers, a student group perhaps, or a television audience, although Mailer believes his play too strong for the latter. He protests that in the television medium with its endless "surface detail . . . fundamental distinctions between the safe and the insecure, the reality and the dream, are marinated, dramatic opposition are bypassed—powerful conflicts are first modulated, then mashed into one another. The side effect is nausea" (*DPP*, pp. 23-24). He considers an actor's job to be "not to provoke emotion, but to bring you in on a reaction" (*DPP*, p. 22). McLuhan would insist that the cool medium of television is responsible for such a reaction, while I would argue that an actor may "hot up" the medium considerably. As far as *The Deer Park* is concerned, however, the medium seems out of joint with the intended message.

Mailer's only other experimentation with theatre to date is a one-act play based on *Why Are We in Vietnam?*, originally called *D.J.* and included in his most recent miscellany, *Existential Errands*, as *A Fragment from Vietnam*. It had a few performances in Provincetown in the summer of 1967. The play consists primarily of narrative or expository speeches by D.J., with additional dialogue with his mother, Hallie, and her psychiatrist, Rothenberg. The play does not depend on special effects, but on theme, characterization, and conflict. The purpose of this play seems to be to experiment with the form of material Mailer had presented in another genre, and to center attention on the interrelationships of the three characters.

Two more experiments in media occur in the year of *Why Are We in Vietnam?*, the first of which is of minimal significance. A book entitled *The Bullfight: A Photographic Narrative with Text by Norman Mailer* is issued along with a phonograph recording of Mailer reading his introductory essay. The idea, one assumes, is that while one looks at the professional photographs of bullfights, the recorded voice gives animation to the pictures, thus creating a third dimension of perception from the combination of the visual and auditory. I could obtain only the book, however, and found the effect of reading words meant to be spoken similar to that of reading John Barth's collection, *Lost in the Funhouse*, intended as mixed media and yet issued simply as a printed book.

Aside from being an experiment in combining media (for the essay was originally printed in *Playboy*), *The Bullfight* is Mailer's elliptical equivalent to *Death in the Afternoon*. Admitting that "it would be memorable not to sound like Hemingway,"[7] Mailer nevertheless echoes Papa's *afición* for the aesthetics of bullfighting. To Mailer a bullfighter is, of course, a potential existential hero who must display extraordinary courage against a worthy opponent in a situation whose outcome is unknown but dangerous. In addition a good bullfight provides a catharsis for the spectators. Mailer describes his own catharsis which involved learning about "the mystery of form" from the style and character of each good bullfighter. One particular matador styled "El Loco" because he was at his worst unspeakably bad and unsurpassed at his best, "spoke of the great distance a man can go from the worst in himself to the best, and that finally is what the bullfight could be all about," that "a man cannot be judged by what he is every day, but only in his greatest moment, for that is the moment when he shows what he was intended to be" (*The Bullfight*, p. 214). (This comment will shed light on the mock heroics of *The Armies of the Night*.) Although thematically developmental, this essay must be said to have limited appeal in the form of its publication in *The Bullfight*, because nonaficionados do not learn the aesthetics of bullfighting, which depends so much on the beauty of movement, from still photographs.

A more significant experiment with form was Mailer's first venture in filmmaking. The philosophy behind this film, predictably, is existentialism à la Mailer. Writing about *Wild 90* in the December 1967 issue of *Esquire*, Mailer contrasts his film to a Hollywood production: Hollywood had been "part of the beginning of the computerized, unionized technological programmed torturing of talent which a generation of electronic guitars has come to take for granted as Salvation Through Chemicals."[8] Further, "the process of commercial film-making has a natural tendency to liquidate the collective human entity of the film"[9]—actors read lines they didn't write and move and gesture in manners prescribed by the director. Mailer's idea centers around actors as existentialists: "if existentialism is ultimately concerned with the philosophy of danger and the attractions of the unknown, acting is one of the surviving rituals of invocation, repetition, and ceremony—of propitiation to the gods."[10] Since the outcome of our actions is unknown, acting which depends upon scripts and elaborate settings is mere role playing. In *Wild 90*, therefore, there is no script. Mailer as producer-director selected a few friends to appear in the film with him—for he is actor too—and gave them the situation out of which they were to develop action. Mailer also directed the cameramen, called for retakes, and edited the completed film. He has controlled its distribution as well.[11] Mailer feels that his experiment in existential filmmaking was successful. Out of the given situation, that of three hoodlums holed up in a room for twenty-one days, conflict began to develop not out of plot nor from the opposition of hero and villain, but "from that more complex opposition which is natural to every social breath of manner, that primary if subtler conflict which comes from trying to sell your idea in company when others are trying to deny you."[12] From the point of view of the audience—and Mailer gives us this appraisal too, making his control of the film as complete as possible—the film has "the most repetitive pervasive obscenity of any film ever made for public or even underground consumption" and so repels many viewers, but yet "tough guys" like the film because it is "filled with nothing so much as [their] vanities, bluffs, ego-supports, and downright collapses of front."[13] Obscenity invites total physical participation in the medium which transmits it, McLuhan tells us, and it is no wonder that when the highly literate person, used to the "hot" medium of the printed page, is drawn into such participation he is repelled.[14] Mailer's concern with self-imposed or collective censorship is that it destroys vitality. His aim in using obscenity in *Wild 90* as later in *Why Are We in Vietnam?* is to produce a "robust art" which "feed[s] audiences with the marrow of its honest presence" and gives "light and definition and blasts of fresh air to the corners of the world."[15]

Although an innovation in concept, *Wild 90* is a film no one but a student of Mailer or of film could be persuaded to sit through twice. The film's dialogue does not appear particularly obscene by current standards, and because it does not startle, it bores. Filmed in sixteen-millimeter black and white, the movie features Mailer and two friends (who, like most of the rest of the cast, appear in his other films too), Mickey Knox and Buzz Farbar, as the "Maf boys," who get on each other's nerves as they wait in their hotel room for the heat to be off. There are occasional visits from family, fellow gangsters and "the bulls," and at the end, reached arbitrarily, Mailer addresses the audience (as he will do in his other films) briefly on the nature of existential filmmaking, and the cast is introduced.

The film's chief virtue and defect derive from the same cause. Since there is no prescribed dialogue, no inevitability to the outcome, much of the film is simply boring, without direction or meaning. On the other hand, by the end of the ninety minutes of footage, something in the roots of the relationship between the three men has been exposed, which, it seems, is what the film is all about. The relationship of the criminals to the police, one of constant fascination to Mailer and the subject of his next film, *Beyond the Law*, belongs as well to that species of "subtler conflict" where manners rather than radical opposites are confronted.

The film is not humorless, if only because of the performance which Mailer gives as a pugnacious, preening hoodlum, full of hot air and an inflated sense of self-importance. His accents and his posturings are exaggeratedly self-conscious and at times hilarious.

Technically, *Wild 90* is amateurish. The sound track is hard to follow and at times inaudible. The camera work is directionless and commits the grossest kind of error which normally ends up on the cutting room floor. Some scene changes are announced by the type of card reminiscent of silent films, reading Another Day, Another Night. Others are unannounced.

Wild 90, therefore, is interesting as a new concept in film and in comparison to Mailer's later, more sophisticated attempts at filmmaking, but it has little intrinsic merit.

Why Are We in Vietnam?, Mailer's last published work of fiction, reveals the distance he has come in the understanding of media since writing *An American Dream.* His subject is what he had referred to in "The Political Economy of Time" as "the spirit of the total corporation" (*CC*, p. 356), which he believes produced that malignant form called the Vietnam War. His medium is voice-print, a kind of silent tape recording which utilizes obscenity, punning, and a style which suggests the patter of a mad disc jockey coming over the airwaves of America, blocking out all other stations while he is on the air. D.J.'s role as disc jockey represents a media breakthrough rather than one in point of view, for D.J. is descended from Mikey Lovett in *Barbary Shore* and the other fictional first-person dramatized narrator-participants through Stephen Rojack. He particularly resembles the narrator in "Advertisements for Myself on the Way Out," because he suggests alternate identities for himself, thus deliberately creating ambiguities concerning his moral nature.

As disc jockey, D.J.'s medium is the radio and the airwaves which transmit his voice. As narrator of a novel, his medium is print. To combine the two, to make a permanent record of a voice, is to record the voice on tape. Although not an actual tape recording, the narrative voice demands that the reader imagine it so. D.J. suggests the possibility that his voice print will become the property of the "electronic Lord" who is keeper of all stored information; and because D.J. cannot identify Him as holy or demonic, his own purpose is ambiguous.

We do not hear D.J.'s voice, but we imagine it. It is strident as a whining microphone to the mind's ear; it acts more as an extension of the central nervous system than of the eye. The voice establishes a private communication with the reader-listener like a radio with an earphone. There is never any letup in the patter; if D.J. needs time to find a phrase, he fills in with nonsense and punning, and his stream of consciousness is not private but meant to be broadcast:

> We're going to tell you what it's all about. Go go, Dr. Jek tell the folk, we're here to rock, the world is going shazam, hahray, harout, fart in my toot, air we breathe is the prez, present dent, and God has always wanted more from man than man has wished to give him. Zig a zig a zig. That is why we live in dread of God.[16]

The total effect of the voice is best described by Mailer himself:

> The words come out in squeaks, spiced with static, sex coiled up with technology like a scream on the radar. Bombarded with his language, the sensation is like being in a room where three radios, two television sets, stereo hi-fi, a pornographic movie, and two automatic dishwashers are working at once while a mad scientist conducts the dials to squeeze out the maximum disturbance. (*CC*, p. 117)

This is how Mailer had described four years earlier the effect on him of Burroughs's style in *Naked Lunch*. At that time Mailer was also disturbed by the fragmented nature of the book, not understanding that the book's style was Burroughs's response to the "senders," equivalent to Mailer's totalitarians, whose messages are designed to achieve ultimate control over the human consciousness. By breaking up their messages, Burroughs nullifies their language and becomes a sender himself, but one who would alter human consciousness for the better.[17] Mailer's similar intentions are a matter of record, and by 1967 he adds his footnote to Burroughs in D.J.: even one whose intentions to control others are good may himself be unknowingly subservient to evil forces, like the America whose ostensible purpose in Vietnam is to free her people for self-determination. Since neither D.J. nor Mailer can know the outcome of his efforts to alter consciousness, the novel is in a sense a self-parody,

114

for it questions the legitimacy of its own undertaking. At the same time it derives its legitimacy from its exposure of its methods, as seen in this early passage.

> America, this is your own wandering troubadour brought right up to date, here to sell America its new handbook on how to live, how to live in this Electrox Edison world, all programmed out, Pronozo! (this last being the name King Alonso gave to the Spanish royal condom.) Well, Huckleberry Finn is here to set you straight, and his asshole ain't itching, right? so listen to my words, One World, it's here for adolescents and overthirties—you'll know what it's all about when you and me are done. (*Vietnam*, p. 6)

Mailer has pulled out all the stops in his effort to communicate with that mass audience frozen in front of their television sets who elected Lyndon Johnson to the presidency and who condoned the violent war they watched on the six o'clock news.

Having realized that a possible way to break the power of "technology land" is to use its means for one's own ends, Mailer by the nature of his style in *Why Are We in Vietnam?* holds our attention from beginning to end. Yet many of his literate readers found that style outrageous, particularly because one of its major devices is obscenity. One reviewer accidently hit upon the point of the book during a vituperative outpouring: "Constipated by indignation at the admittedly dreadful war, Mailer's ['customers'] bless any purgative by calling the result a novel."[18] Using hunted animals as a metaphor for the Vietnamese, Mailer tells us that we are in Vietnam because it is a convenient purgative for our national violence which when suppressed will lead to suicide. And Mailer's novel is an attempt to expose that purgative as one which substitutes madness for suicide and to prescribe a purgative offering relief from both: obscenity. As John Aldridge, one of the novel's most sympathetic critics, has put it: *Why Are We in Vietnam?* can "be seen as telling us something important not only about the obscenity of our situation in Vietnam, but far more crucially, about the possible power of obscenity to help alleviate that situation."[19]

Ever since his army experience, Mailer has been fascinated with the power of obscenity to cleanse. For him it is linked to his admiration for the principle of American democracy and the American language. He tells us in *The Armies of the Night* that having discovered in the Army "the democratic principle with its faith in the common man," he came to believe that

> that noble common man was as obscene as an old goat, and his obscenity was what saved him. The sanity of said common democratic man was in his humor, his humor was in his obscenity. And his philosophy as well—a reductive philosophy which looked to restore the hard edge of proportion to the overblown values overhanging each small military existence. . . . Mailer never felt more like an American than when he was naturally obscene—all the gifts of the American language came out in the happy play of obscenity upon concept, which enabled one to go back to concept again. . . . So after years of keeping obscene language off to one corner of his work, as if to prove after *The Naked and the Dead* that he had many an arrow in his literary quiver—he had kicked goodbye in his novel *Why Are We in Vietnam?* to the old literary corset of good taste, letting his sense of language play on obscenity as freely as it wished, so discovering that everything he knew about the American language (with its incommensurable resources) went flying in and out of the line of his prose with the happiest beating of wings—it was the first time his style seemed at once very American to him and very literary in the best way. (*Armies*, p. 62)

He goes on to say that "obscenity probably resides in the quick conversion of excitement to nausea" (ibid.), and if we add to this a statement made earlier, that "being half excited and half frustrated leads to violence" (*CC*, p. 196), the purgative nature of obscenity and Mailer's advocacy of it as an alternative to Vietnam becomes clear.

Appropriately, the obscenity in *Why Are We in Vietnam?* is anal in nature. From "The Time of Her Time" and the first scene with Ruta in *An American Dream*, we have learned that the anal is associated with the Satanic. The higher the grade of the "asshole" the more Satanic is his nature, and the more difficult it is for the average man to recognize him as such, because he is very much a part of the established power structure. A medium-grade asshole (or M.A.!) is a junior executive who will ascend to a higher grade through the perverted Horatio Alger method: through lying, cheating, and destroying the competition. D.J.'s father, Rusty Jethroe, is the "highest grade of asshole made in America and so suggests D.J.'s future: success will stimulate you to suffocate!" (*Vietnam*, p. 38). "Success" in business in Mailer's scheme is equivalent to "success" in Vietnam, and in the novel's particular metaphor, "success" in hunting. When Rusty takes credit for killing a bear which was rightly D.J.'s in order to achieve status, the corruption inherent in the American Dream of success is neatly exposed.

The ambiguities of identity with which D.J. invests himself, that is, whether he is a "Harlem spade," or hipster, or a Texas Wasp (which is to say a murderer, for Johnson was born and Kennedy died in the state) are the result of his parentage. A metaphor for America's future, D.J. must learn to overcome the burdens of his past. His father representing America at its technological worst, D.J.'s mother Hallie is a stereotypical castrating female. Worse, she is representative of America's schizophrenia: a "lady" because she suppresses verbal obscenity and "just thinks that way" (p. 21). The identity problem is symptomatic of the larger "ambiguity at the center of D.J.'s message center" (pp. 50–51), the black and white, good and evil ambiguity in terms of which Mailer sees America. Although D.J. is able to see "right through shit" (p. 50), he is unsure of the source of his perception and is afraid that what he sees will craze him as the animals of the Brooks range have been crazed by contact with technological hunting, and as his father has become crazed by the lust to kill.

The motif of the hunt, which others have recognized as the "classic American myth tale of quest, initiation, and ultimate absolution" with the demonic at work beneath an idyllic surface,[20] and the even closer parallels to Faulkner's "The Bear" and a number of Hemingway's works,[21] becomes invested with more than ritual significance in Mailer's novel. D.J.'s suppressed violence toward his father must find an outlet or turn to cancer. In a hunt conducted by professional guides with the aid of helicopters and high-

117

powered rifles, man has so perverted the ethics of hunting as to become more bestial than the animals he hunts—and the parallels Mailer intends to the nature of the Vietnam War are obvious. Since World War II America has not combatted a foreign enemy equal to its strength, and hunting lesser game produces not growth but madness. The hunt conducted by D.J. and his alter ego, Tex Hyde, (the Jekyll/ Hyde dichotomy runs through their relationship) is for an equal enemy. By stripping themselves of illegitimate aids, they begin to perform an ancient "purification ceremony" of a good kill. Moving beyond "The Bear" and its many predecessors in American literature, this hunt takes place on America's last frontier: the white expanses of the Alaskan North, which in Mailer's scheme is the repository of all human knowledge present in the electromagnetic force field of the North Pole. The hunt therefore takes on Faustian implications. Entering the force field where no human had set foot, the boys experience an electric charge which excites them with a lust to kill. They oversee a fight between a white wolf and an eagle (metaphorically madness versus America) which is a cowardly draw. They evade the helicopters searching for them and, cleansed of "mixed shit," enter bear country. Having left their weapons behind, they cannot kill the bear they encounter there, although D.J. senses that "the center of all significant knowledge" (*Vietnam*, p. 207) would be revealed to him by the bear's death, as in Faulkner's story. Instead D.J. watches the bear kill a caribou and takes away the secret that there is "no peace in the North" (p. 211).

That night, still electrified with frustrated violence, the boys wake to the Aurora Borealis. Each is filled with a lust to sodomize the other—the Satanic implications are clear—but suppresses the desire because he knows the other will kill him. It is then that their initiation takes place, coming not in a vision (the method of *An American Dream*) but through electrified airwaves, as if all of the violence of the continent were concentrated in the Brooks Range:

118

. . . they hung there each of them on the knife of the divide in all
conflict of lust to own the other yet in fear of being killed by the
other and as the hour went by and the lights shifted, something in
the radiance of the North went into them, and owned their fear,
some communion of telepathies and new powers, and they were
twins, never to be near as lovers again, but killer brothers, owned by
something, prince of darkness, lord of light, they did not know;
they just knew telepathy was on them, they had been touched forever by the North and each bit a drop of blood from his own finger
and touched them across and met, blood to blood, while the lights
pulsated and glow of Arctic night was on the snow, and the deep
beast whispering Fulfill my will, go forth and kill, and they left an
hour later in the dark to go back to camp and knew on the way each
mood of emotion building in Rusty and Big Luke and Ollie and M.A.
Bill and Pete and their faces were etched just as they had foreseen
them and the older men's voices were filled with the same specific
mix of mixed old shit which they had heard before in the telepathic
vaults of their new Brooks Range electrified mind. (*Vietnam*, pp.
219-20)

The revelation which accompanies their initiation is that
their God is a beast, a killer. Using a symbol which equates
God with a malign whiteness, as Poe, Melville, and Frost had
done, Mailer's terrifying message, delivered here in Faulknerian rhythms, is that man's fate is God's fate: in becoming more evil, man remakes God in his own image. "God is
like Me, only more so," the narrator of "Advertisements for
Myself on the Way Out" told us (*Adv.*, p. 493), and America's God in this apocalyptic vision is Satanic. "You never
know what vision has been humping you through the
night," D.J. concludes as he and Tex are off to Vietnam
(*Vietnam*, p. 224). Although the question asked in the novel's title has been answered, the central ambiguity which it
raised remains. Is D.J.'s future, as America's, to be decided
in a glorified Armageddon known as Vietnam? The book's
vision is Mailer's prophecy of America's fate should she
continue in her present direction. D.J. is no hero but a victim as America is a victim of the American Dream.

As for the book's style, it suggests an alternative guide to
the one America and Tex and D.J. have been following. By
blocking out all competitive airwaves for the length of time it

takes us to complete the book, by offering the essentially comic purgative of obscenity rather than the tragic purgative of war, by parodying the use of language to control consciousness, Mailer created a novel successful in its own aesthetics if not in its intended immediate effects. Long-range effects, such as the influence of the novel's ideas or language, are of course unpredictable.

One Mailer critic, Barry H. Leeds, contends that *Why Are We in Vietnam?* suffers from a lack of integration of the political message, system of metaphor (a carryover from *An American Dream* in his opinion and therefore invalid for *Vietnam*), and narrative voice.[22] His reading points up the difficulty of applying textual analysis to the book: one is forced to pry it loose from its context and try to objectively evaluate the harmony of its parts. *Why Are We in Vietnam?* does not lend itself to such analysis because it is designed to set the reader's teeth on edge, to jar him out of his complacency, to *change* him by its power to communicate. In other words, the reaction of the reader is a key part of the book. The question of the novel's success or failure, it seems to me, must rest upon whether Mailer has been true or false to his own aesthetics, whether the book represents progress or a regression, and whether it reveals or conceals a little more of the mystery of human existence. The novel registers growth in three areas: one, it extends the flow of mainstream American literature by revealing something more to us of our national character than we have known before, particularly as it applies to America's participation in her most controversial war of this century; two, by offering a purgative to insanity, murder, and suicide through the explosive humor of obscenity to put together the America we have rather than to look for a new one, as Stephen Rojack was made to do; and three, by inventing a style to cut through the deadening effects of the mass media. Although we cannot measure the effect of Mailer's book nor of his ideas on the war which continued for some years to drain America's physical, economic, and spiritual resources, we can consider the novel in the contexts it was intended to modify.

The Armies of the Night

The Product: The Armies of the Night

> To the ostent of the senses and eyes, I know, the influences which stamp the world's history are wars, uprisings or downfalls of dynasties, changeful movements of trade, important inventions, navigation, military or civil governments, advent of powerful personalities, conquerors, etc. These of course play their part; yet, it may be, a single new thought, imagination, abstract principle, even literary style, fit for the time, put in shape by some great literatus, and projected among mankind, may duly cause changes, growths, removals, greater than the longest and bloodiest war, or the most stupendous merely political, dynastic, or commercial overturn.[23]

The vision of the "great literatus" is Whitman's a century ago and, with reservations, Mailer's today. The most significant statement that Mailer has made to date on the possible effectiveness of the artist is contained in *The Armies of the Night*, subtitled *History as a Novel/The Novel as History*. What Mailer has been able to do in *The Armies of the Night* is literally to make history. He has made a metaphor of his participation in a protest against the Vietnam War and has himself become the object of his long search for an authentic American hero. Further, as a consequence, Mailer has had to come to terms with the significance and effectiveness of such a hero in our time. In these ways and others, *The Armies of the Night* is the culmination of not only the prolific and diversified output of work since *An American Dream*, but also, more than anything else he has written, a product, that is, the final result of a long process discernible in the product itself.

Two of the major concerns of Mailer's art over the years, the search for a hero and for an effective style for that hero, are solved in *The Armies of the Night*. We remember from *The Presidential Papers* that the main requirement of Mailer's hero is that he be capable of uniting in himself the two rivers of American life, the mundane and the dream of the extraordinary. In *Advertisements for Myself*, the hipster was suggested as a possible hero but later rejected because he could represent only one extreme. The Mailer of *Advertisements for Myself* was able to see his role as that of the creator of a viable hero but knew that he himself was not ready to fill

121

the role. The demise of Mailer's personally selected flesh-and-blood hero, Jack Kennedy, propelled him to create a fictional possibility in Stephen Rojack. But Rojack proved both too extraordinary and too weak, capable only of constructing a new America of radical possibility, a dream of an America where presumably the mundane would have no place. Similarly D.J. is too ambiguous a character to be considered heroic; nor is he his own man. Mailer's own assumption of the heroic role may well have been inevitable since neither his real nor his fictional protagonists passed the crucial test.

To become his own representative hero Mailer had to pass not one but two tests: he had to synthesize in himself the commonplace and the extraordinary, possible only through experiencing the synthesis as the outcome of a significant antithetical action; and he had to find a way to convert subjectivity to objectivity, to make himself a "literary object." I quoted earlier from his review of Norman Podhoretz's *Making It*, published at the same time as *The Armies of the Night* and so presumably written somewhat concurrently, in which Mailer analyzed the difficulty of creating a character of oneself.[24] The "worst of the difficulty" as Mailer sees it is that

> one is forced to examine oneself existentially, perceive oneself in the act of perceiving, (but worse—far worse—through the act of perceiving, perceive a Self who may manage to represent the separate warring selves by a Style). It is necessary to voyage through the fluorescent underground of the mind, that arena of self-consciousness where Sartre grappled with the *pour-soi* and the *en-soi*: intellections consuming flesh, consciousness the negation, yes, the very consumption of being. One is digesting one's own gut in such an endeavor.[25]

Presumably the necessary agonizing has been undergone successfully between the experiencing of the events of October 1967 and the writing of them in *The Armies of the Night*. The narrator is separate from the participant in this book as is evidenced by the former's referring to the latter as "Mailer." In the three novels following *The Naked and the Dead*, it will be remembered, Mailer used a first-person narrator-protagonist identifiably separate from the implied author. In

Why Are We in Vietnam?, D.J., although similar to these narrators in every other respect, refers to himself in the third person. The transition from the first-person narrator-protagonist as a separate persona of the implied author is made in *The Armies of the Night*. The "Mailer" who has acted is distinct from the Mailer who is writing, the latter having assimilated the experiences of the former and, having done so, gone beyond him. Such a method of distancing the one self from the other accounts in part for the essentially comic, deflating tone used of "Mailer."

As already mentioned, the hero was to synthesize the common man with his ideal self. A key to the mock-heroic "Mailer" of the early chapters of *The Armies of the Night* may be found in the essay "The Crazy One," first published in *Playboy* in October 1967 and entitled "A Footnote to Death in the Afternoon" when reprinted as the introduction to *The Bullfight*. We remember the matador in the essay, "El Loco," whose style was either dreadful or glorious and who to Mailer "spoke of the great distance a man can go from the worst in himself to the best," illustrated that "a man cannot be judged by what he is every day, but only in his greatest moment, for that is the moment when he shows what he was intended to be."[26] In these terms it is clear that Mailer's aesthetics of heroism depend on the establishment of the hero first as a man whose link with commonalty lies in the beast in his nature, in his capability for degradation of the self so that, by contrast, his small victories over his baseness become triumphs, truly heroic because they have overcome so much. It is with this concept in mind that the narrator of *The Armies of the Night* subjects us to a lengthy account of the events of the evening preceding the march on the Pentagon. At a pre-rally dinner Mailer makes known his wish to act as master of ceremonies for the evening's program. Reaching the theatre where the rally is to be held, Mailer goes off in search of the men's room. Full of bourbon and an inflated sense of his oratorical abilities, he attempts to use the urinal without turning on the lights. He misses. Some minutes later he enters the theatre hall only to discover that someone has usurped his position

123

as emcee. He insists on taking over. His ramblings and obscenity produce jeers, exasperation, and disgust in his audience. Our mock-hero has succeeded in bringing out the beast
in himself.

It is against this incident that all of Mailer's later actions
which bear on the march will be measured. What, then, is the
nature of Mailer's heroism in the book? It centers around his
perception that one is not permitted to confront the power at
the top in the United States as Rojack could confront Kelly in
An American Dream. Who, then, was the potential American
hero to confront and attempt to defeat: a couple of terrified
National Guardsmen, a United States marshal, a commis-
sioner who would teach him a lesson by confining him to jail,
the press who inevitably misquote him? Taken separately
these opponents hardly approximate a Barney Kelly. Even
combined they are scarcely fit foes for a romantic hero. While
standing in the cold October air as man after man stepped
forward to make his symbolic gesture against the war by
presenting his draft card for burning, Mailer felt threatened
by the pitiful inadequacy of such gestures:

> . . . As if some final cherished rare innocence of childhood still pre-
> served intact in him was brought finally to the surface and there ex-
> pired, so he lost at that instant the last secret delight he retained in life
> as a game where finally you never got hurt if you played the game well
> enough. For years he had envisioned himself in some final cataclysm,
> as an underground leader in the city, or a guerrilla with a gun in the
> hills, and had scorned the organizational aspects of revolution, the
> speeches, mimeograph machines, the hard dull forging of new parties
> and programs, the dull manoeuvering to keep power, the intolerable
> obedience required before the over-all intellectual necessities of each
> objective period, and had scorned it, yes, had spit at it, and perhaps
> had been right, certainly had been right, such revolutions were the
> womb and cradle of technology land, no the revolutionary truth was a
> gun in the hills, and that would not be his, he would be too old by then,
> and too incompetent, yes, too incompetent said the new modesty, and
> too showboat, too lacking in essential judgement—besides, he was too
> well-known! He would pay for the pleasure of his notoriety in the im-
> possibility of disguise. No gun in the hills, no taste for organization,
> no, he was a figure-head, and therefore he was expendable, said the
> new modesty—not a future leader, but a future victim; *there* would be
> his real value. (*Armies*, p. 94)

124

Not a leader but a victim, not to manipulate but to be manipulated—this was the chief ambiguity surrounding D.J.'s fate and the center of Rojack's dread. And yet the Mailer who narrates has grown beyond the Mailer watching the draft dodgers and the author of *An American Dream* and *Why Are We in Vietnam?* He realizes that like Christ or John F. Kennedy a man may be both leader and victim—a martyr; that in fact one's willingness to be victimized, to attract the attention of the powers at the top, invests one with a charisma, a sense of having been touched by magic, and one's confrontations then, however insignificant they may appear, become magnified by the aura of mystery and power which surrounds the man into battles worthy of Saint George. To openly identify oneself as an enemy of the Establishment exposes one to the punative means at its disposal, particularly likely to be invoked when the powerful are under heavy attack. For this reason and in contrast to his former degradation, Mailer's act of forcing a military policeman to arrest him for crossing a police line, physically dangerous in itself, takes on mighty proportions. Following his arrest,

> He felt as if he were being confirmed. (After twenty years of radical opinions, he was finally under arrest for a real cause.) Mailer always supposed he had felt important and unimportant in about as many ways as a man could feel; now he felt important in a new way. He felt his own age, forty-four, felt it as if he were finally one age, not seven, felt as if he were a solid embodiment of bone, muscle, flesh, and vested substance, rather than the heart, mind, and sentiment to be a man, as if he had arrived, as if this picayune arrest had been his Rubicon. (*Armies*, p. 157)

Having taken great risk, the rewards are great. In this way, Mailer found not only a means of making a representative American hero of himself but also a way to combat power that would remain faceless and so unassailable. In *The Armies of the Night* Norman Mailer becomes a counterforce both literally and metaphorically to totalitarianism.

Mailer further establishes the heroism of symbolic action by means of several contrasts based on the impotence of words and actions whose ends are predictable. Between himself and Robert Lowell, Mailer develops the contrast of authentic and inauthentic heroism. Lowell, the descendent of a long line of distinguished American litterateurs and statesmen, has the aura of a prince while next to him Mailer appears a buffoon. But yet it proves that the prince is less effective than the buffoon: Lowell foregoes arrest to return to New York to host a dinner party; Mailer, although regrettably, misses the party in order to go to jail. If Lowell wishes to be a hero, Mailer suggests that he earn the right:

> You, Lowell, beloved poet of many, what do you know of the dirt and the dark deliveries of the necessary? What do you know of dignity hard-achieved, and dignity lost through innocence, and dignity lost by sacrifice for a cause one cannot name. What do you know about getting fat against your will and turning into a clown of an arriviste baron when you would rather be an eagle or a count, or rarest of all, some natural aristocrat from these damned democratic states. No, the only subject we share, you and I, is that species of perception which shows that if we are not very loyal to our unendurable and most exigent inner light, then some day we may burn. (*Armies*, p. 54)

Lowell represents too the suicidal direction of American life and the impotence of tradition: the "natural aristocrat," inheritor of her most upheld tradition of working for change within the system, now is outspokenly opposed to the policies of the Establishment and condones the breaking of what he considers her unjust laws, but yet is himself, to Mailer's lights, ineffective in bringing about change.

Another contrast centers around the innumerable speeches made in the three-day period of the march. Speech after speech dulled whatever inflammation might have resulted from any one man's words. The rhetoric of the march came to represent to Mailer a kind of verbal diarrhea, like the rhetoric of the Johnson administration. Yet Mailer feels that he himself is a good extemporaneous speaker and is somewhat insulted when not asked to speak at every gathering. To him the relationship of speaking to acting should be one of cause and effect: one's words inspire action. We recognize this as part of his philosophy and of his concept of leadership. This is why the speeches of potential leaders like Lowell, although they contain the right words, fail because the speakers do not follow them with significant action, in this case being arrested and therefore consciously forcing the power structure to deal with one's opposition.

Other contrasts are drawn between the methods of certain power groups within the march. Mailer compares the Old Left, to which he once owed allegiance, to the New Left, which includes all those who organize to change the Establishment. The Old Left, according to Mailer, based its revolution on the "sound-as-brickwork-logic-of-the-next-step" (*Armies*, p. 102), while the New Left's "aesthetic" is existential: it "began with the notion that the authority could not comprehend nor contain nor finally manage to control any political action whose end is unknown" (pp. 104–5). And yet the New Left is essentially dull, while the Old Left had an imaginative sense of apocalypse. Not only does Mailer support his own principles by these contrasts, he also considers the diversity of the participants in the March and their interactions with each other and with government negotiators to be "a paradigm of the disproportions and contradictions of the twentieth-century itself" (p. 255). If the march is a metaphor for our time, the dynamic interaction of the diverse forces should produce a new synthesis for our time, and Mailer's concept of the synthesis is present in the form of his book and in his own role as hero.

Based on a chronological account of his participation in the events surrounding the march on the Pentagon, Mailer's new synthesis is seen unfolding in book one of *The Armies of the Night*. The action of book one as a whole may be seen as "Mailer's" progress from the mock-heroic to the heroic through the increasing significance of his confrontations. The space between these encounters, by revealing that a man can be a buffoon one moment and a hero the next, gives added significance to those existential moments when one's courage is tested. This plot line, constructed on factual incidents with interpretations by the Novelist, forms the basis for the synthesis of "history as a novel." The reasons for the emergence of the new style are clarified in the following passage. Observing a busload of America's children on their way to the March, Mailer broods on the power the mass media have exerted on them and on the waning influence of America's novelists:

> A part of him had always tried to believe that the America he saw in family television dramas did not exist, had no power—as of course he knew it did—to direct the styles and the manners and therefore the ideas of America (for in a country where everyone lived so close to their senses, then style, precisely, and manner, precisely, carved ideas into the senses) ideas like conformity, cleanliness, America-is-always-right. . . .
>
> . . . As the power of communication grew larger, so the responsibility to educate a nation lapped at the feet, new tide of a new responsibility, and one had become a writer after all to find a warm place where one was safe—responsibility was for the pompous, and the public servants; writers were born to discover wine. It was an old argument and he was worn with it—he had written a good essay once about the failure of any major American novelist to write a major novel which would reach out past the best-seller lists to a major part of that American audience brainwashed by Hollywood, TV, and *Time*. Yes, how much of Fitzgerald's long dark night may have come from that fine winnowing sense in the very fine hair of his nose that the two halves of America were not coming together, and when they failed to touch, all of history might be lost in the divide. Yes, there was a dark night if you had the illusion you could do something about it, and the conviction that not enough had been done. (*Armies*, pp. 177–79)

Although the novelist has the vision, the mass media have the audience. Both have the power to create a world roughly based on facts and to manipulate one's interpretation of those facts. If one believes, as Mailer does, that his interpretations should shape the nation, he must battle for power with opposing interpretations. Mailer overgoes his competitors, the journalists who report the news, in two main ways, first in his role as participant, as protagonist of his own narrative. Like Whitman, Mailer can say, "I am the man, I suffered, I was there." The combination of these roles is rare even in the interpretive journalist. The various titles Mailer assigns to himself during the course of *The Armies of the Night* indicates the growing representativeness of his roles: first only the "Novelist," he becomes in addition "Participant," "Historian," "Beast" (a role assigned to him—unlike novelists, participants can be manipulated), "Romantic," "Master of Ceremonies," "minor poet," "Citizen," "Ruminant," and "Protagonist." Second, Mailer uses the mass media to keep himself in the news. However much his words or actions are misrepresented, he is still getting coverage, and that coverage leads to more with less and less need for its instigation on Mailer's part (interestingly, Mailer reports that his actions during the weekend of the march and notably his arrest were being filmed for a BBC documentary, later entitled "Will the Real Norman Mailer Please Stand Up?"). Applied to the march, the use of the mass media is related to Mailer's concept of growth through existential confrontations: "A protest movement which does not grow loses power every day, since protest movements depend upon the interest they arouse in the mass media. But the mass media are interested only in processes which are expanding dramatically or collapsing" (*Armies*, p. 259). If one's actions or ideas are meant to influence, one's style must be attention getting. A taste for notoriety and an inflated ego have been taken for granted as the motives for his controversial actions, even by admirers of his writing. It should now be clear that his public performances, while less aesthetically satisfying than his written work, proceed in the main from the same motivation, the alteration of the contemporary consciousness. The media have consistently focused public attention on the extremes in his behavior and his writing, and he has had a tendency to combat this in extreme ways, compounding the public's illusion that his is a radical, even a violent personality.

Having established that the main reasons for Mailer's style in *The Armies of the Night* were to communicate all of the nuances and the ultimate significance of the march on the Pentagon to a mass audience, to substitute his style for that of the mass media, and in so doing to make a representative American hero of himself, let us look more closely at his new style and the subjects of his attacks.

Mailer opens the book with an account in *Time* magazine of his participation in events preceding the march. One knows the type of article: it is more concerned with being witty and provocative than with being factual and unbiased. Without commenting on the story, Mailer undercuts it with this remark: "Now we may leave *Time* in order to find out what happened" (*Armies*, p. 14). Finding out what *really* happened has long been the province of the journalist or historian. Mailer's question concerning the validity of their accounts is how one can know the truth if one has not experienced it or if one does not share the novelist's gift of intuition and his feeling for nuance. Further, Mailer believes that journalists and historians are incapable of handling the ambiguous. Here is Mailer's justification for his approach.

> The March on the Pentagon was an ambiguous event whose essential value or absurdity may not be established for ten or twenty years, or indeed ever. So to place the real principals, the founders or designers of the March . . . in the center of our portrait could prove misleading. They were serious men, devoted to hard detailed work; their position in these affairs, precisely because it was central, can resolve nothing of the ambiguity. For that, an eyewitness who is a participant but not a vested partisan is required, further he must be not only involved, but ambiguous in his own proportions, a comic hero, which is to say, one cannot happily resolve the emphasis of the category—is he finally comic, a ludicrous figure with mock-heroic associations; or is he not unheroic, and therefore embedded somewhat tragically in the comic? Or is he both at once, and all at once? These questions, which probably are not much more answerable than the very ambiguities of the event, at least help to recapture the precise feel of the ambiguity of the event and its monumental disproportions. Mailer is a figure of monumental disproportions and so serves willy-nilly as the bridge—many will say the *pons asinorum*—into the crazy house, the crazy mansion, of that historic moment when a mass of the citizenry—not much more than a mob—marched on a bastion which symbolized the military might of the Republic, marching not to capture it, but to wound it *symbolically*. . . . So if the event took place in one of the crazy mansions, or indeed *the* crazy house of history, it is fitting that any ambiguous comic hero of such history should be not only off very much to the side of the history, but that he should be an egotist of the most startling misproportions, outrageously and often unhappily self-assertive, yet in command of a detachment classic in severity (for he was a novelist and so in need of studying every last lineament of the fine, the noble, the frantic, and the foolish in others and in himself). Such egotism being two-headed, thrusting itself forward the better to study itself, finds itself therefore at home in a house of mirrors,

> since it has habits, even the talent to regard itself. Once History inhabits a crazy house, egotism may be the last tool left to History. (*Armies*, pp. 67-68)

So the quality of Mailer's performance in *The Armies of the Night* depends on his ability to bridge the gap between the mock-heroic and the heroic. We noted earlier the beastly behavior which established the low point on the scale for measuring Mailer's heroics, while the high point came through his most significant action, transgressing, with some foreknowledge of the danger and consequences, the line of military police guarding the Pentagon. Some of the intermediate gradations on the scale, with fluctuations, illustrate the nature not only of Mailer as hero but also by extension the potential for heroism which resides in each of us.

Following his arrest Mailer wonders how long he will be jailed. Naïvely he supposes that he will be released in time to make Lowell's dinner party. After all, his object was to be arrested, he had made his point, and that, he thought, was that. Hours later the inexperienced participant is enlightened by his alter ego, the knowing "Novelist":

> Why had he expected the government to be crisp, modest, and pleasantly efficient in their processing of Pentagon prisoners? "Because ass," he said to himself, "they have brainwashed you as well." And it was true. The only reason he had expected to be out of jail in half an hour was the covert impression he had of government as brotherly; dull but brotherly; ten thousand hours of television, ten million words of newsprint added up to one thundering misapprehension of all the little details of institutional life. (*Armies*, p. 182)

The noble Mailer plans to fast throughout his term in jail. And yet before the thought has settled, he takes a drink of water. He seems to himself either "saint" or "debauchee" with "no middle ground ... tenable for his appetite" (p. 185).

The "saint" begins to hand out the money in his wallet to pay the prisoners' fines, but the "debauchee" holds back the money from those he does not like and of course saves out enough for himself. At every turn he, like the America he has come to believe he personifies, is divided between the thought and the act, the justification and the manifestation, the good and the evil. How to put it together and make the good outweigh the evil? This the crucial question, Mailer finds a way. While in jail he listens to a student radical incite the prisoners to further protest and envisions prison as

> an endless ladder of moral challenges. Each time he climbed a step . . . another higher, more dangerous, more disadvantageous step would present itself. Sooner or later, you would have to descend. It did not matter how high you climbed. The first step down in a failure of nerve always presented the same kind of moral nausea. . . . To become less guilty, then weaken enough to return to guilt was somehow worse than to remain cemented in your guilt. (*Armies*, p. 219)

Through this metaphorical expression of his concept of existential growth or failure, as in the earlier passage quoted (*Armies*, p. 94), Mailer, with his new experience, reassesses his method of evaluating his existential battles: perhaps one ascends the moral ladder not rung by rung equivalent to each action but by an accumulation of positive acts which outweigh the negative. This important knowledge comes as, free at last from jail, Mailer realizes how his rather linear interpretation of one's moral development can imprison him.

> He felt a liberation from the unending disciplines of that moral ladder whose rungs he had counted in the dormitory . . . no, all effort was not the same, and to eject oneself from guilt might yet be worth it, for the nausea on return to guilt could conceivably prove less: standing on the grass, he felt one suspicion of a whole man closer to that freedom from dread which occupied the inner drama of his years, yes, one image closer than when he had come to Washington four days ago. The sum of what he had done that he considered good outweighed the dull sum of his omissions these same four days. So he was happy, and it occurred to him that this clean sense of himself, with a skin of compassion at such rare moment for all . . . it must come crashing soon, but still—this nice anticipation of the very next moves of life itself . . . must mean, indeed could mean nothing else to Christians, but what they must signify when they spoke of Christ within them, it was not unlike the rare sweet of a clean loving tear not dropped, still held. (*Armies*, p. 238)

Comparing this mature Mailer to Rojack at the end of *An American Dream*, we can see the distance he has come. America's hero is not Superman but a very human being who with courage can summon up enough nobility on occasion to rise above himself, to outweigh his failures, although because he is human he will fail again. This knowledge is what makes him a "whole man" by uniting the ordinary self with the dream self and can by extension make America a whole nation.

With his philosophy and art having been unified through the establishment of himself as the metaphorical American, the Novelist's work in *The Armies of the Night* is complete. By virtue of one's interest in this "Mailer," book one is by far the more important, and indeed is three-fourths of the book's whole. Too, the second book suffers from its placement, for because it is less interesting it is anticlimactic. And yet it is a vital part of Mailer's account of the march. As the emphasis in the first part has been on history as a novel, so in the second part it is on the novel as history; that is, the unified sensibility having been established, it will now apply itself to the events of the march. As Mailer expresses it:

> The mass media which surrounded the March on the Pentagon created a forest of inaccuracy which would blind the efforts of an historian; our novel has provided us with the possibility, no, even the instrument to view our facts and conceivably study them in that field of light a labor of lens-grinding has produced. (*Armies*, pp. 245–46)

Mailer's virtue in book two is not that he offers an objective view of the events, but that he does not pretend to. His "history" is a combination of personal experience and eyewitness accounts culled from all manner of sources, not weighed for their accuracy as might be expected in a history, but filtered through a central intelligence. Mailer explains his method.

> . . . history is interior—no documents can give sufficient intimation: the novel must replace history at precisely that point where experience is sufficiently emotional, spiritual, psychical, moral, existential, or supernatural to expose the fact that the historian in pursuing the experience would be obliged to quit the clearly demarcated limits of historic inquiry. So these limits are now relinquished. The collective novel which follows, while still written in the cloak of an historic style, and, therefore, continuously attempting to be scrupulous to the welter of a hundred confusing and opposed facts, will now unashamedly enter that world of strange light and intuitive speculation which is the novel. (*Armies*, p. 284)

Mailer was not the first novelist of his generation to create a hybrid through the crossbreeding of contemporary event with fictional mode. Truman Capote some years earlier published *In Cold Blood* with much the same rationale: that the novelist's imaginative insight can rend truth from a set of bare facts. Similarly, John Hersey has for a number of years worked with the same genre in books like *Hiroshima* and *The Algiers Motel Incident.* Mailer's central contribution to this hybrid form has been his presence at the creation of the events he writes about, so that not only are his facts as carefully and thoroughly researched as those of Capote and Hersey, but his participation has in subtle ways borne on the substance of the facts. In another direction, the strong personal style which is characteristic of Mailer's essays allies him with another contemporary whose points of view on contemporary culture are thrust upon us through a heavily foregrounded style, Tom Wolfe. Through the efforts of such men in recent years the demarcations of journalistic writing have been significantly expanded.

The final test Mailer's method must pass is whether it reveals to us more of the shape of events surrounding the march on the Pentagon than what we know from the conventional sources available to us. As we have come to expect, Mailer expresses his concept of the events as a metaphor. What the march finally comes to mean for him may be seen in the final lines of Matthew Arnold's "Dover Beach" to which the title of Mailer's book alludes:

> . . . the world, which seems
> To lie before us like a land of dreams,
> So various, so beautiful, so new,
> Hath really neither joy, nor love, nor light,
> Nor certitude, nor peace, nor help for pain;
> And we are here as on a darkling plain
> Swept with confused alarms of struggle and flight,
> Where ignorant armies clash by night.
>
> (Ll. 30-37)

As in this anguished vision of the end of security and faith and the emergence of a terrifying new age of uncertainty, Mailer sees the march as another struggle to preserve the old

134

faith in the American Dream and one with its measure of success. The march has analogues in all of America's struggles: the Revolutionary and Civil Wars and the Old Left movement of the thirties are emphasized, and all are seen as "rites of passage" for the participants, either positive or negative in nature. "Men learn in a negative rite to give up the best things they were born with, and forever" (*Armies*, p. 316) and in a positive rite of passage to hold on to those things at all costs. Those who participated in support of the Vietnam War, all depicted as members of the military, police, or government, took the negative rite, Mailer believes. Like the language of "technologese," they succeeded in "stripping [themselves] of any moral content" (p. 315). And what of the others, the other ignorant army? Even the worst of these, the "spoiled children of a dead de-animalized middle class" were forced to make a positive passage by "moving . . . to a confrontation they could only fear" (pp. 311–12). The best, perhaps, were those highest on the moral ladders, the Quakers and pacifists who remained in jail rather than compromise: "who was to say that the sins of America were not by their witness a tithe remitted?" (p. 319) Diverse though they may be, these opponents of the Establishment herald that new revolution in consciousness which Mailer has long sought and which Charles Reich has recently depicted as "Consciousness III" in *The Greening of America*. The aim of the new consciousness is the transcendence of technology by making the machine enrich rather than impoverish human life, to make America green again. This, ultimately, is the aim of Mailer's book, as its final page makes clear. We must deliver America from her bonds, because "we must end on the road to that mystery where courage, death, and the dream of love give promise of sleep" (*Armies*, p. 320).

Whether or not one agrees with his moral assignments of the sides, one must acknowledge that Mailer's interpretation of the march has imparted to it a form and an urgency unmatched in other accounts. *The Armies of the Night* more than any other of Mailer's works illustrates the value of his theory of existential growth, applied through a representative hero to the potential growth of the nation. It unites and balances through a new maturity the separate parts of that aesthetics: Mailer's life, his art, his ambitions, and his vision. The self-advertisement he had learned from Hemingway is tempered by the humility and wisdom of this book's spiritual father, Henry Adams. Like Adams's account of the interaction of the self with history, Mailer's "education" has resulted in a broadening of his horizons, as well as those of the novel, the autobiography, journalism, and history by combining these various ways of viewing reality in *The Armies of the Night*. Warner Berthoff has noted that the book is also a reinvention of "a classic American literary mode: the exploratory personal testament in which the writer describes how he has turned his own life into a practical moral experiment and put it out at wager according to the chances, and against the odds, peculiar to the public character of his time and circumstance."[27] Berthoff compares *The Armies of the Night* to the autobiographies of Ben Franklin and Lincoln Steffens and particularly to Thoreau's *Walden*. The similarities are there. However, I think we can see an essential difference, one that argues for Mailer's creation of a new synthetic form, that is to say, that Mailer's intention throughout his experiences with the anti–Vietnam War movement was to push the pro–Vietnam War forces out of shape by the strength of his own will and consequently acts consciously as representative hero not only for his readers but for those present at that time, including the BBC crew filming a Mailer documentary. Mailer had foresight as well as hindsight concerning the significance of his role in the march on the Pentagon.

In recognition of his achievement and in consideration of his abiding concern for the fate of America, he was awarded by the cultural Establishment he opposes their two highest awards for *The Armies of the Night*: the 1968 National Book Award for arts and letters and the Pulitzer Prize in general nonfiction.

The Armies of the Night

NOTES

1. These books are *Miami and the Siege of Chicago, Of a Fire on the Moon, The Prisoner of Sex, St. George and the Godfather, Marilyn, The Faith of Graffiti,* and *The Fight.*
2. Robert W. Lawler, "Norman Mailer," p. 156.
3. Norman Mailer, *The Armies of the Night,* p. 33. All further references are cited in the text, and the title will be shortened to *Armies.*
4. Norman Mailer, *The Deer Park: A Play,* p. 12. All further references are cited in the text, and the title will be shortened to *DPP.*
5. John Olsen Stark, "Norman Mailer's Work from 1963 to 1968," p. 162.
6. Gerald Weales, *The Jumping-Off Place,* p. 221.
7. Norman Mailer, "The Crazy One," p. 91.
8. Norman Mailer, "Some Dirt in the Talk," p. 193.
9. Ibid., p. 194.
10. Ibid.
11. This film as well as *Maidstone* and the two versions of *Beyond the Law* are available through New Line Cinema, 121 University Place, New York, New York 10003, which also handles Mailer's public appearances.
12. Mailer, "Some Dirt in the Talk," p. 267.
13. Ibid., p. 190.
14. Marshall McLuhan, *Understanding Media,* p. 44.
15. Mailer, "Some Dirt in the Talk," p. 269.
16. Norman Mailer, *Why Are We in Vietnam?,* p. 7. All further references are cited in the text, and the title will be shortened to *Vietnam.*
17. I am indebted to Tony Tanner's discussion of Burroughs in *City of Words,* pp. 109-40.
18. Charles T. Samuels, "The Novel, USA: Mailerrhea," p. 406.
19. John W. Aldridge, "From Vietnam to Obscenity," p. 91.
20. Ibid., p. 92.
21. Barry Leeds, *The Structured Vision of Norman Mailer,* pp. 182 and 187-88.
22. Ibid., p. 203.
23. Walt Whitman, "Democratic Vistas," p. 366.
24. Norman Mailer, "Up the Family Tree."
25. Ibid., pp. 240-41.
26. Mailer, "The Crazy One," p. 214.
27. Warner Berthoff, "Witness and Testament," p. 189.

IN THE CENTER OF HISTORY

With the establishment of himself as participant in and interpreter of contemporary American events in *The Armies of the Night*, Mailer's conception of his role as the instrument and director of change comes to fruition. His work following *Armies* is dependent upon his right to this role; if we do not accept the authority of his voice, we cannot accept his ideas and interpretations. Even admirers of Mailer's books, however, have been unable to reconcile with the writing what they consider such perversities as his New York mayoralty campaign, his conviction that he is a major opponent of the Women's Liberation movement, and certain of his more colorful public appearances, notably his fiftieth birthday party. By now it is clear that while Mailer is less effective in certain media and at certain events than others, his motivations in undertaking them are of a piece. One of his favorite quotations is Voltaire's "Once a philosopher, twice a pervert." In an effort not to repeat himself and to continue growing, Mailer has done a number of things which do not enhance his reputation as a major writer. Once we recognize that his existentialism underlies all of his efforts, it becomes easier to sort out their relative merits and to deal with Mailer as a whole.

Having made himself, at least in his work, an American spokesman-hero, Mailer is obliged to confront those events which have the capability of influencing our national destiny. His active participation where possible and, lately, his research of areas not previously known to him, lend vitality to his perspectives. He exerts on such events whatever force is possible in an effort to affect the shape of the future. His greatest fear seems to be that humanism will be phased out as the electronic age phases out traditional literary forms. Perhaps what is most heroic about Mailer's efforts is his continued participation in the monumental battle for human control and transcendence of the inevitable scientific and technological advancements. Mailer knows that "being a hero is an existential state. It can vanish in a season," because a hero is someone who "embod[ies] some spirit of the time. . . . A man can be a hero only for a very short time, unless he is really in the center of that history that's moving on and on and on."[1] He literally placed himself at the center of history in *The Armies of the Night* and his interest in political events and cultural phenomena has kept him there ever since.

A most interesting part of his ongoing dramatic dialectic was his campaign for the Democratic Party's nomination for the office of mayor of New York in the spring of 1969. Mailer was willing to set aside writing for an active political role, a tangible means of putting his theories into practice. The campaign is the subject of two books, *Managing Mailer*, by Joe Flaherty, and Peter Manso's *Running against the Machine*, both written or edited by young men who were actively involved in his campaign. Mailer ran as a "left conservative," a characteristic synthesis of extremes which he described this way: left conservatism

> insists that politics be an extension of our personal lives and that existence is nothing if not for individual responsibility and action. At bottom it requires every man to gauge the success or failure of his life by the extent to which he knows that life and all that it might be. It calls for democracy but a democracy which is nothing if not pluralistic. In effect, it is everything that the center is not.[2]

The main plank in Mailer's platform was that New York become the fifty-first state. It would then be free from a crippling economic dependence upon Albany and able to develop its own great potential. The city-state would reorganize itself into independent neighborhoods with the power to conduct their own affairs:

> Power to the neighborhoods would mean that any neighborhood could constitute itself on any principle, whether spiritual, emotional, economical, ideological or idealistic. . . . Life in the kind of neighborhood which contains one's belief of a possible society is a form of marriage between one's social philosophy and one's private contract with the world.[3]

The idea is intriguing but depends upon a kind of frontier spirit that has been all but bred out of Americans. However, the contention that the revival of that spirit is the means toward any future America might develop is a long-standing belief of Mailer's. This essentially conservative element in his "left conservatism" is dominant in the following excerpt from a campaign essay.

> . . . the old confidence that the problems of our life were roughly equal to our abilities has been lost. Our authority has been handed over to the federal power . . . we cannot forge our destiny. So our condition is spiritless. We wait for abstract impersonal powers to save us, we despise the abstractness of those powers, we loathe ourselves for our own apathy. . . . Who is to say that the religious heart is not right to think the need of every man and woman alive may be to die in a state of grace, a grace which for atheists and agnostics may reside in the basic art of having done one's best, of having found some part of the destiny to approach, and having worked for the view of it?[4]

In this essay Mailer is not far from espousing the Protestant ethic. To this conservatism with its emphasis on individualism and the spiritual rewards of hard work is conjoined the liberal tradition of working for change within the existing machinery of the system. Thus the concept of "left conservatism" embraces the two greatest traditions in American political life: cooperative government designed to promote creative individualism.

However attractive or visionary Mailer's position papers might have been to certain voters (he polled 41,136 votes, his running mate nearly twice that),[5] he proved no practical politician, making all the mistakes a politician can make to lose

In the Center of History

votes: he was late for appointments; he offended the press by constantly reminding them of his superior stature as a writer (his Pulitzer Prize for *The Armies of the Night* was announced on May 6, soon after the campaign began); he offended both members of his own staff and potential contributors; he used obscenity at political gatherings;[6] he chose as a running mate a man, Jimmy Breslin, whose public image emphasized the idiosyncracies of his own and caused the press to treat them as a comedy team, and worst of all, by his own assessment, he was forced to endlessly repeat himself, creating a void between his words and his aesthetics.

While the campaign failed of its goal by a great margin, it was nonetheless a growth experience for Mailer. Near the beginning of his first book following the campaign, *Of a Fire on the Moon*, he assesses the personal effects of his political venture.

> He came in fourth in a field of five, and politics was behind him. He had run, when he considered it, no very remarkable race. He had obviously not had any apocalyptic ability to rustle up large numbers of votes. He had in fact been left with a huge boredom about himself. He was weary of his own voice, own face, person, persona, will, ideas, speeches, and general sense of importance. He felt not unhappy, mildly depressed, somewhat used up, wise, tolerant, sad, void of vanity, even had a hint of humility. (*Fire*, pp. 5-6)

If the mayoralty campaign may be said to constitute an experiment in nonliterary communication, one in which content was sacrificed to a noncomplementary style, or in which Mailer did not travel the distance from the worst in himself to the best, his continued experiments with "existential" filmmaking explored style as content. *Beyond the Law*, filmed in 1967 and released in 1968, and *Maidstone*, made in the summer of 1968 and released in 1970, were similar in conception to *Wild 90*. Mailer again assumed the roles of actor, producer, director, and editor and chose from among his friends and acquaintances to act out a central idea. *Beyond the Law*, a film about "cops and robbers," is based on Mailer's concept that schizophrenia is the modern disease, and that those such as policemen and criminals who seek outlets for violence demonstrate by how thin a tissue our society is held together. The policeman and the criminal are two halves of a whole, Mailer contends, in this film which traces the after-hours activities of three off-duty policemen. Having such an idea to explore stylistically in the film represents an advancement beyond *Wild 90*, which was concerned solely with making film a medium of existential style.

There are two versions of *Beyond the Law: Red* and *Blue*. *Red* was the original, while *Blue* was recut and substantially changed in its conclusion by Mailer. As in *Wild 90*, Mailer, Buzz Farbar, and Mickey Knox have the leading roles, this time as Police Lieutenant Francis X. Pope and two of his detectives. The supporting cast is large and includes José Torres, Rip Torn, Beverly Bentley (Mailer's fourth wife), and George Plimpton in a cameo role as New York's Ivy League mayor. The structure of the film is fairly simple: Rocco Gibraltar (Farbar) and Mickey Berk (Knox) meet two girls in a restaurant and recount their day in a series of flashbacks, during which we meet and follow through interrogation a lineup of suspects. Near the end of the film, Pope's meeting with his wife in another restaurant is juxtaposed to that of the detectives, and when Mrs. Pope announces that she has committed adultery with Gibraltar, Pope seeks him out. Having assured himself that his wife has lied, Pope asks Lee Ray Rogers, an attractive brunette prostitute whom he interrogated that day, to join him and the detectives. In the *Red* version of the film, she is driven away by Pope's wife, and Pope and the detectives philosophize on cops and criminals, addressing the audience directly in the last scene. In *Beyond the Law—Blue*, after Mrs. Pope drives Rogers and the detectives' dates away, Gibraltar and Berk go to Rogers's apartment, where Gibraltar photographs her having intercourse with Berk. Then for spite they show Pope the pictures. Later the same evening Pope goes to her apartment for some existential sex and the film ends as did the *Red* version with the three cops in a bar, and Pope breaking down the film's illusion by addressing the audience. The only other significant difference between the two versions is that in *Blue* narrative continuity during the interrogations of suspects gives way to more rapid and more frequent juxtapositions of scenes.

As for the substance of the film, it makes the point, which Mailer has made elsewhere, that although criminals and police are on opposite sides of the law, they are more alike than different. The criminals generally resemble a "brave and witty set of self-creations" (*PP*, p. 16) while the police tend to be totalitarians. But there are no "good guys" and "bad guys," only the morally ambiguous. Pope, as his name suggests, symbol of authority and rather humorously pompous, a kind of Mailer self-parody, tells one spaced-out hippy who uses the phrase "God's asshole" that "God and asshole are the essence of criminality. You mix the two and it's the beginning of all evil." In another scene he informs a suspect that there are three reasons to pursue evil: to defeat it, to collaborate with it, or because one is apathetic about it. Believing himself to have been doing the first, in the final scene with Lee Ray Rogers in *Blue* Pope seems to be collaborating with it, placing himself in jeopardy beyond the law where he, like Stephen Rojack, learns that one must experience evil in order to combat it. Indeed, the film resembles *An American Dream* as it might be told from Lieutenant Roberts's point of view, and among the criminals is a man who killed his wife because he "wanted to find out who [he] was."

In some of the interrogations lie the possibilities of existential filmmaking. Peter Rosoff, for example, is excellent as a respectable man accused of soliciting in a subway station who manages to preserve his dignity against all attempts by the police to break it down. Effrontery seems to be the chief means of defense by any suspect against the fascistic methods of the police. Because there is no script, the actors seem to come closer to the edge of subconscious revelation than in conventional drama; the actors are authors as well. Mailer keeps fairly tight reins on the film's structure, giving the actors enough latitude to unearth some real drama in the conflicts between victims and police, yet retaining the necessary threads of continuity. The *Blue* version makes more thematic sense than the *Red* in terms of Pope's situation and is a film interesting in itself as well as for its innovations.

Technically also, *Beyond the Law* is superior to *Wild 90*. We still find some rough camera work (the cameras are held by hand and frequently in the wrong place at the right time), and some hard-to-catch dialogue, but there is more going on, more life to the film, and consequently a greater challenge to film well. *Beyond the Law* bears some resemblances to ciné-ma vérité work such as John Cassavetes's *Faces*, both in technique and intention, the major difference being that Mailer uses actors who are improvising rather than people who are playing themselves. *Beyond the Law* received a few reviews but little serious attention. Like Mailer's other films it has not had commercial distribution and is available through a single agency.

Mailer's third film, *Maidstone*, received considerable advance publicity. The accounts given in the *New York Times* exemplify the kind of coverage Mailer typically receives for his nonliterary performances and reveal why it is that admirers of Mailer's writing find his public image difficult to reconcile with the writing. The first article, entitled "Norman Mailer Enlists His Private Army to Act in Film," undercuts Mailer's serious intentions in making the film by creating the impression that it is a lark or an orgy. An orgy it may have been for some, for that was part of the film's latitude, but a lark it was not. Mailer gathered a large group of friends, associates, and technicians on four Long Island estates to try to make a film in five days. A *Times* photo shows him orienting the group on the nature of the film while the caption reads, "Norman Mailer . . . explains to models, playwrights, social figures and others what the 'beautiful, tasteful, touching, evocative' movie is about. It's about a director, played by Norman Mailer."[7]

The second *Times* article, by the same journalist, appears eight days later under these headlines: "Mailer Film Party a Real Bash: 1 Broken Jaw, 2 Bloody Heads." The incident which, finally, gave the film its raison d'être, an existential fight between Mailer and actor Rip Torn, is presented as crude and irresponsible violence, irrespective of its context within the film.[8]

Another article appears in the *Times* two years later upon the release of *Maidstone* in London. The headlines again emphasize Mailer as pugilist: "Mailer, in London, Trades Jabs with Audience over New Film." The point of the article is that the film's sophisticated audience correctly panned it while Mailer egotistically defended its concepts. Here is the opening paragraph: "Norman Mailer took a pounding from young British film enthusiasts this week over his new, loose-gaited motion picture called 'Maidstone.' Mr. Mailer told his critics they would like his picture better if they saw it 10 times."[9]

Maidstone is a much more ambitious film than the previous two. The size of the cast and crew, the lavish settings, the hefty budget, the use of color film all contributed to the impression that Mailer was going to try to outdo himself again. Filmed in June of 1968, just a few weeks after Robert Kennedy's assassination, an atmosphere increasingly tense and full of dread grew out of the interplay of the actors. The situation which Mailer designed for the film, centering around Norman T. Kingsley (Mailer's middle name), famous film director and presidential candidate ripe for assassination, encouraged the potentially violent atmosphere.

Filming took place over a period of a week with little time out for sleep. Camera crews often operated without direction, as did the actors—a mélange of amateurs, professionals, Mailer's friends and acquaintances, including four of his five wives, and no doubt some curiosity seekers. While certain scenes were structured by Mailer, neither their outcomes nor that of the film as a whole was prescribed, so that the film's structure is developed at two levels: by the actors themselves, both with and without Mailer's direction, and by the cutting of the film on which Mailer spent nearly two years following the filming. *Maidstone*'s ending provides the logical conclusion to both structural levels. Kingsley (Mailer) is surrounded by a circle of friends (several quite literally Mailer's friends: Buzz Farbar, José Torres, Eddie Bonetti, Rip Torn) known as the Cashbox, dominated by Kingsley's half-brother, Raul Rey, played by Torn. Rey is described as "a man about whom there is not only enigma but a certain proclivity toward malevolence."[10] A secret police organization known as PAX,C (Prevention of Assassination Experiments, Control), ambiguous as to whether it prevents or promotes assassinations, appears to have approached Rey to assassinate Kingsley. A "Grand Assassination Ball" takes place during which both Mailer and Kingsley anticipate violence which does not occur. The sequence before this, the surrealistic "Death of the Director," anticipates both the Assassination Ball and the film's conclusion. The ball, whatever its outcome, was to have ended the film proper and was followed, as was the case with Mailer's earlier films, with Mailer the actor turned to Mailer the director addressing his audience, this time the cast, on the nature of the film. He told them that he felt that the film "would all come together one way or another" when he saw the rushes and began cutting. Rip Torn muttered, "You may have some surprises" (*Maidstone*, p. 118). What followed brought to culmination and significance both the film itself and Mailer's theories of existential filmmaking: as Mailer watches several of his children play in a field, Torn approaches him with a hammer in hand and strikes him several blows on the head, explaining, "You're supposed to die, Mr. Kingsley. You must die, not Mailer, I don't want to kill Mailer, but I must kill Kingsley in this picture" (*Maidstone*, p. 121). The two men grapple while Mailer's wife and children watch, horrified, and the cameras continue to roll. After they break off Torn tries to convince Mailer that "the picture doesn't make sense without this," to which Mailer replies, "It was my picture, and I knew what I was doing with it, and what makes sense, and what don't" (p. 127). And yet Torn (although witnesses are convinced that he actually tried to murder Mailer), not Mailer, determined the film's conclusion, one precipitated by its violent context and within that context totally logical. Through the attack, in which the roles of Raul Rey and Norman T. Kingsley were confused with the real relationship between Torn and Mailer, *Maidstone* succeeded in becoming a film about the nature of reality, both "the surface of reality and the less visible surface of psychological reality" (p. 178). Torn's attempt to destroy the hero he admired is also strangely like the murder of Mailer by the young revolutionary in Alan Lelchuk's *American Mischief.* There is something peculiarly American present in these literal and fictional attempts to bring down the king of the hill.

The confusion of the two levels of reality became, ultimately, *Maidstone's* aesthetic base and its subject. In his essay "A Course in Filmmaking," we find that Mailer's explorations into the nature of film relate closely to his own aims as an artist: to bring portions of the subconscious to light in order to unite actuality with the dream and as a consequence to order what had been chaotic. We recall a line from "The Man Who Studied Yoga" in which Sam Slovoda remarks, "Kill time and chaos may be ordered" (*Adv.*, p. 173) and find this statement in the *Maidstone* book: "We look at film, any film, and chaos is to a degree ordered" (p. 171). Chaos seems to reside in the uncontrollable shifts of moods and events of which our lives are full: "Film is the art of controlling those shifts, revealing relationships among them: film is the only art which can search, cut by cut, into the mystery of moods which follow and accommodate one another; film is the only art which can study sudden shifts of mood which sever that ongoing river of time a fine film has set in flow (*Maidstone*, pp. 179–80). Film is also the art, Mailer contends, through which transcendence is possible. There are moments, of which Rip Torn's attack is the quintessence, when "a psychological reality in the mind . . . transcends itself and becomes a fact" (p. 171). Indeed, the film would not have worked without that particular moment, which elevated it from merely an interesting film to a significant one.

Clearly, filmmaking is an important aesthetic extension of Mailer's existentialism. *Maidstone* brought together the threads initiated in *Wild 90* and *Beyond the Law* and is the only one of these to have a logical conclusion. It is a film

147

which would be difficult for Mailer to outdo, although his work in this area warrants further development.[11] *Maidstone* often accompanies him on the college circuit; it is a visible achievement.

If few have had an opportunity to view the film, Mailer has ensured that they may read about it in *Maidstone: A Mystery*, published in October 1971, which includes "A Combined Account of the Filming of *Maidstone*" from three sources, which, typically, is countered at the book's conclusion by Mailer's own in "A Course in Filmmaking." In between lies the screenplay of *Maidstone*, taken from the soundtrack, to which Mailer has added descriptive comments to indicate mood and expression. In effect, the book interprets, even rewrites, the film for us, as if we could not comprehend *Maidstone* without it, and certainly as if Mailer must create the film's significance in the absence of critical acclaim.

His credentials as film critic in order, Mailer reviewed a controversial film which received much acclaim, Bertolucci's *Last Tango in Paris*.[12] It is not well known that Mailer spent part of 1949 to 1950 in Hollywood working on movie treatments, and that his fascination with film and film stars is long standing. The central flaw of *Last Tango*, he quite rightly observed, was that it offered only half a loaf: the end of the film was given, but the actors were encouraged to improvise. Improvisation engages all of an actor's resources; if he is good he takes risks, so that he as well as his fellow actors and his audience discovers something about himself. Had Brando and Schneider been allowed to take their improvisations with each other where they led, we might have been given a truly great film, one that broke through the barriers of artificiality, as *Maidstone* had begun to do.

The years since the filming of *Maidstone* have brought about a significant change in Mailer's position with respect to the Establishment. Having received its major literary awards, he is cautiously accepted as a member of the club (each of his new books is reviewed on page one of the *New York Times Book Review*), although, as we have said, his extraliterary adventures are still held suspect. His longstanding battle for fair coverage with Time-Life, Inc., resulted in their coming over to his side when he received $450,000 for *Life* magazine's and subsidiary rights to his views on the Apollo 11 flight. Big money also came his way for magazine rights to books such as *Miami and the Siege of Chicago, The Prisoner of Sex, St. George and the Godfather,* and *Marilyn.* One Mailer critic, John Stark, expressed concern that Mailer may have sold out to the Establishment by accepting their assignments and accepting them for such huge sums.[13] However, readers of these books can rest assured that Mailer pays no homage to Time-Life; on the contrary, he is using them to disseminate his views. My only reservation is that magazine deadlines leave little time for reflection and revision. The urgency to get his material in print (particularly the two books on the political conventions which came out a matter of weeks after the conventions, barely in time to exert whatever influence they could on the outcome of the presidential elections) must be weighed against whatever the books lose from such haste. Certainly Mailer looks upon his journalistic assignments as a challenge; they involve a greater risk in one respect than his more carefully written work, for they force him to produce the best work he can at top speed, and some of it is very good indeed. We are reminded that *An American Dream* was first written in monthly installments for *Esquire* and, although considerably revised and improved before hardcover publication, the novel's essence remained unchanged. On the other hand, as Mailer put it in *The Faith of Graffiti,* "Journalism is Chores. Journalism is bondage unless you can see yourself as a private eye inquiring into the mysteries of a new phenomenon."[14] Thus Mailer justifies the journalistic work which has occupied him almost exclusively in recent years because a novelist's perception and intuition is required for "truth" to emerge from the event, while still considering his "longest ball" the novel that he announced in 1959 that he would write and on which he is now working. The books on contemporary events have had priority over the novel, partly because they can be written quickly and are lucrative, partly because Mailer is attracted to those events which "have a magnetic relation to [his] own ideas,"[15] but the novel may be his magnum opus.

Linked to his recent journalistic efforts to influence our view of the present are Mailer's frequent public appearances, several on late-night "talk" shows. During an engagement on "The Dick Cavett Show" (October 7, 1971), Mailer boxed three very respectable rounds with former light-heavyweight boxing champion José Torres, who taught Mailer to box in exchange for being taught how to write. Boxing has long been an interest of Mailer's as it was for Hemingway, for it in every way expresses his concept of existentialism. Never missing an opportunity to score a point, during that same program he offered an opinion on what he considered to be Governor Rockefeller's inept handling of the Attica prison riot and suggested an alternative prison system.

A year later, on October 26, 1972, Mailer appeared, for the second time, on "The Johnny Carson Show" to promote *St. George and the Godfather* and to comment on the presidential candidates. On that occasion he was more solemn than vitriolic, as audiences seem to expect him to be and as he had been in the well-known exchange with Gore Vidal over Mailer's theory of violence on Cavett's show on December 1, 1971. Richard Poirier, after considering Mailer's performance on the latter evening, concluded that "where Mailer is not, by virtue of the act of writing, able to control a situation, the hidden thrust of his energy is toward the sacrificial waste of himself."[16] While I agree with Poirier (although not with his onanistic imagery) that, given the nature of television talk shows, Mailer has gained little in that medium, this is not true of other of Mailer's public performances, nor can it be said, as I have been arguing, of his extraliterary work as a whole. I have attended three of Mailer's university speaking engagements and have seen him work hard to gain ground with an audience, shifting tactics to become attuned with the mood of the group or to shatter it.[17] His style I would term "existential polemics," designed with the same purpose as his other work: provoking a response in his audience through dialectics, pushing them closer to his own position or closer to a void in their own. And he is generous of himself with these groups, remaining to answer questions or to sign autographs long after other speakers would have decided that the audience had gotten its money's worth. When he can't get through to an audience he claims it as his own fault and is disappointed, for he has a sense of himself at his best which he works at outdoing.

A well-known example of his failure to bring off a performance occurred on the occasion of his fiftieth birthday party, held on February 1, 1973, at the Four Seasons restaurant in New York. Approximately 550 guests, many famous figures from politics, sports, and the arts, paying $50 per couple, attended the party at which Mailer was to make an announcement of "national importance (major)" about the Fifth Estate.[18] The Fifth Estate was to be the people's equivalent of the CIA or FBI to investigate conspiracies such as the assassinations of the Kennedys, Martin Luther King, Malcolm X, the shooting of George Wallace, and—with an uncanny timeliness—the Watergate break-in. The organization was also to train a citizen's intelligentsia in investigatory methods of broad applicability. Support of all kinds was to be sought from the wealthy and powerful guests. Something went wrong in the presentation of the idea, however, and Mailer, characteristically, criticized his own performance: "the speech was a disgrace. It had neither wit nor life—it was perhaps the worst speech on a real occasion that the orator ever made." He goes on to suggest that in the "indifference" and "apathy" present in his own voice on that occasion he had moved nearer to "the national character,"[19] and I would suggest closer to the Mailer of *The Armies of the Night* whose emceeing of the anti–Vietnam War rally was a similar disgrace. It is through the writing of this defense of the idea while criticizing his performance that Mailer wished to regain some ground for the Fifth Estate. After months of seeking support for the organization and trying to interest college students in forming their own investigatory chapters, to little avail, Mailer arranged for the merger of the Fifth Estate with a similar group called CARIC (Committee for Action/ Research on the Intelligence Community).

The risk involved in trying to manipulate voters or a live audience keeps Mailer close to the existential edge of himself. If this extraliterary work bears little fruit directly, it at least keeps Mailer in shape for the existential battles he wages with himself and his subjects in his writing. It probably will prove that his writing does contain his most effective and enduring efforts. An examination of Mailer's books since *The Armies of the Night* will enable us to see the direction his writing is presently taking and provide some perspective on the three major works I have already discussed.

Miami and the Siege of Chicago was written not only against a publisher's deadline but against Mailer's own objective of publication prior to the 1968 presidential election in order to influence that election. Unlike his 1960 essay, "Superman Comes to the Supermarket," written to help elect John Kennedy, *Miami and the Siege of Chicago* does not so much promote a candidate as a point of view. Mailer once again makes himself the representative American through whose actions the Republican and Democratic conventions are illumined.

We may consider the book in two lights: as a product of Mailer's interaction with specific events and as a part of the continuing process of his life and art. These two perspectives conflict somewhat, with the consequence that *Miami and the Siege of Chicago* is not so good a book as *The Armies of the Night*. Central to the conflict is Mailer's conception of his role in interpreting the events of the summer of 1968. As a "reporter" with a contract from *Harper's* magazine to fulfill and press credentials which make him one of a large corps of reporters at the conventions, Mailer is obliged to allow the presidential contenders center stage rather than himself. Of course it is expected that he will evolve a unique interpretation based on his own philosophical principles. Yet we do not expect a reporter to be an active participant. No reporter in *The Armies of the Night*, Mailer depended in his narration upon his prior participation. Reporting excludes participation as narrating does not, and a nonactive role is not Mailer's strongest position.

In part one, "Nixon in Miami," Mailer is strictly an interpretive, though imaginative, journalist. He first establishes the place of the Republican convention, Miami Beach, as a metaphoric American Hell: a tropical climate "transmogrified by technological climate" and "the materialistic capital of the world."[20] Next the Republican presidential contenders are described in language that both deflates by style and inflates by implication their importance. They are for Mailer the faces of Wasp power in America. Only Nixon is an enigma to "the reporter." His previous impressions of Nixon are horrific:

> There had been a gap between the man who spoke and the man who lived behind the speaker which offered every clue of schizophrenia in the American public if they failed to recognize the void within the presentation. Worse. There was unity only in the way the complacency of the voice matched the complacency of the ideas. (*Miami*, p. 42)

Now Nixon gives the reporter evidence that he has "some knowledge of the abyss" (p. 44), the essential quality Kennedy had lacked. The current enigma Nixon presented was

> whether he was a serious man on the path of returning to his own true seriousness, out to unite the nation again as he promised with every remark ... or whether the young devil had reconstituted himself into a more consummate devil, Old Scratch as a modern Abe Lincoln of modesty. (*Miami*, p. 47)

In other words, is Nixon an agent of good or evil? This is the ultimate ambiguity to which Mailer sooner or later elevates any show of power. His obsession with the question provides the book's moral framework and creates the need to examine all facets of Nixon's character for whatever truth it might reveal. The question is at least as interesting for its ironies after Nixon's resignation.

Nixon's evidence of growth since the Eisenhower years and his potential for heroism excite Mailer as "a measure of the not-entirely dead promise of America if a man as opportunistic as the early Nixon could grow in reach and comprehension and stature to become a leader" (*Miami*, p. 50). Mailer is eager that Nixon be what he seems for he could then transfer some of his own weighty role as American hero to Nixon. Mailer's American Dream could be embodied in Richard Nixon:

> To cleanse the gangrenous wounds of a great power, to restore sanity to the psychopathic fevers of the day, to deny the excessive demand, and nourish the real need, to bring a balance to the war of claims, weed the garden of tradition, and show a fine nose for what was splendid in the new, serve as the great educator who might introduce each warring half of the nation to the other, and bring back the faith of other nations to a great nation in adventurous harmony with itself—yes, the dream could be magnificent enough for any world leader; if the reporter did not think that Nixon, poor Nixon, was very likely to flesh such a dream, still he did not know that the attempt should be denied. It was possible, even likely, even necessary, that the Wasp should enter the center of our history again. (*Miami*, p. 62)

It is Mailer's belief that Wasps hold every power in America but "the one they needed—which was to attach their philosophy to history" (p. 52). More and more, American conservatism is coming to express to Mailer the vision lacked by the Left:

> perhaps the Wasp had to come to power in order that he grow up, in order that he take the old primitive root of his life-giving philosophy—which required every man to go through battles, if the world would live, and every woman to bear a child. . . . For certain the world could not be saved by technology or government or genetics, and much of the Left had that still to learn. (*Miami*, p. 63)

This view will prove central to Mailer's next book, *Of a Fire on the Moon.*

Part one of *Miami and the Siege of Chicago* ends as "the reporter stood in the center of the American scene" (p. 63), his now-characteristic position, with his and America's hopes riding on an enigma called Richard Nixon, who still promised something to everyone and spoke like a computer. Mailer's inability to intuit whether Nixon is friend or foe is deflating to his ego and this perhaps is the essential reason for the consistency of his role as reporter in part one.

Part two is a different story. It owes more to the Mailer of

In the Center of History

The Armies of the Night in that the significance of observed events forces him to act. The section is nearly twice as long as part one and gets better and better as Mailer abandons the role of reporter and again becomes novelist-participant.

In contrast to Miami, Mailer sees Chicago as "the great American city" (*Miami*, p. 85), a metaphor for the great energy and potential of America in the nineteenth century before it became diseased, the city that Dreiser wrote about. Mailer devotes three pages to a description of the stockyards and the butchering of hogs, preparing a metaphor for Mayor Daley's "pigs": "Watching the animals be slaughtered, one knows the human case—no matter how close to angel we may become, the butcher is equally there" (p. 89). (John Stark has noted the frequent use of porcine imagery in this section.)[21] A few pages later Mailer relates his having received the news of the shooting of Robert Kennedy. He prays that Kennedy's life be spared, and that he himself be punished for a recent act of adultery, and generally for man's inability to maintain a balance "between the angel in oneself and the swine" (*Miami*, p. 93).

Having reached this low only weeks before the Democratic convention, we look to see what growth experiences Mailer will have to report as his narrative continues. After establishing that Chicago is a vastly more interesting city than Miami Beach, Mailer goes on to attribute a greater dynamism to the Democratic than to the Republican convention. In his view the conflict between the Hawks and the Doves broke the back of the Democratic party. He develops as part of the view the theory of politics as property: each party member holds a piece of property that he bestows upon or withholds from a participating candidate. If one ignores the theory, as McCarthy did by being his own man, he loses the game. Humphrey, on the other hand, was a "small genius" for combining properties that had been antagonistic, such as trade unionism and anticommunism had been before World War II (p. 107). In the end the convention was a struggle for property by the Doves and Hawks, and the most dramatic portions of the struggle took place on the streets of

155

Chicago where the battle between the Hippies, Yippies, and other Doves and Chicago police in Mailer's eyes became the central metaphor for the convention, the Vietnam War, and the mood of the country as it moved into the last third of the twentieth century.

Prior to these events Mailer had been unsure of his courage and of the purposefulness of the large gatherings of antiwar demonstrators in the parks and streets. He compares the events to the Pentagon march.

> The justifications of the March on the Pentagon were not here. The reporter was a literary man—symbol had the power to push him into actions more heroic than himself. . . . The symbol of the Pentagon had been a chalice to hold his fear.
> But in Chicago, there was no symbol for him. (*Miami*, p. 144)

It was not until the police began to clash with the demonstrators that Mailer saw a clear battleground. Playing the role of passive observer, he watches from a hotel window as the Chicago police, taunted by rocks and cries of "Pig," beat the demonstrators. To Mailer the battle is "the murderous paradigm of Vietnam;" it is "history for once . . . taking place . . . on the center of the stage, as if each side had said, 'Here we will have our battle. Here we will win' " (pp. 172-73). The police action gave rise to Mailer's vision of the future as a totalitarian nightmare in which more and more punitive control is administered until all opposition is stilled. This is the mood he saw enveloping the Democratic convention.

Now Mailer's personal reaction to the battle becomes a test of his heroism:

> He liked his life. He wanted it to go on—not as it was going, not Vietnam—but what price was he really willing to pay? Was he ready to give up the pleasures of making his movies, writing his books?
> Where was his true engagement? To be forty-five years old, and have lost a sense of where his loyalties belonged—to the revolution or to the stability of the country (at some painful personal price it could be suggested) was to bring upon himself the anguish of the European intellectual in the Thirties. And the most powerful irony for himself is that he had lived for a dozen empty hopeless years after the second world war with the bitterness, rage, and potential militancy of a real revolutionary, he had had some influence perhaps upon this genera-

156

tion of Yippies now in the street, but no revolution had arisen in the years when he was ready.

These are large thoughts for a reporter to have. Reporters live happily removed from themselves. (*Miami*, p. 188)

This passage is the core of the book and Mailer here stands at the crossroads between his past and his future. All that he has stood for may be opposed to the fruits of his labor. That night while the battle still rages in the streets, Mailer walks among the National Guardsmen, playing his old role of gadfly.

At this point in the narrative, with Mailer once again assuming the role of leader, he breaks off to return to the convention with this explanation:

If this were essentially an account of the reporter's action, it would be interesting to follow him through the chutes on Thursday, but we are concerned with his actions only as they illumine the event of the Republican Convention in Miami, the Democratic Convention in Chicago, and the war of the near streets. (*Miami*, p. 197)

Here Mailer switches from history as a novel to the novel as history, but the transition frustrates the reader who wishes to follow Mailer through the chutes.

At the end of the book Mailer recounts an episode in which he is twice arrested and released for minor confrontations with guardsmen and police, and the experience is renewing:

The fact that he . . . was ready to fight, made him feel close to some presence with a beatific grace . . . and that left him happy, happier than he had been at any moment since he had heard the awful cry of the wounded pig in his throat at the news Bobby Kennedy was shot. (*Miami*, pp. 220–21)

Yet we are not convinced that Mailer's action has been significant nor that the conventions were apocalyptic. The ending is low-key, anticlimactic, disappointing. Again, I believe that the conflicting roles of reporter and novelist-participant as well as Mailer's tendency to inflate the significance of conventions are primarily responsible for the inferiority of *Miami and the Siege of Chicago* to *The Armies of the Night*, although interestingly both were nominated for the National Book Award that *The Armies of the Night* won.

Like *Miami and the Siege of Chicago, Of a Fire on the Moon* was originally written for magazine publication. Portions of the book appeared in *Life* in August and November 1969 and January 1970 before the hardcover edition of the fall of 1970. Also as in *Miami and the Siege of Chicago*, Mailer is an on-the-spot reporter who will provide us with interpretations of the larger significances of the moonshot (a job for which he is uniquely qualified, with his Harvard degree in aeronautical engineering and his Emersonian ability to see the most in the least things); and, as in the previous two books, he sees the event as a paradigm of the twentieth century, with the astronauts representative of American schizophrenia, and the mission as ultimately either divine or satanic. But we can agree that this event has enormous implications, much more so than the political conventions or even the street battle in Chicago. A key to Mailer's assumption of his role as American navigator is found in the following statement: "The horror of the Twentieth Century was the size of each new event, and the paucity of its reverberation" (*Fire*, p. 34). It seems that since *The Armies of the Night* Mailer has taken on the responsibility for creating the necessary reverberations for each event he covers. If he lost somewhat of a sense of proportion in Miami, he has regained it in *Of a Fire on the Moon*, which I consider the finest of the works dealing with contemporary crises since *The Armies of the Night* and a monumental work in itself, whose literary antecedent is *Moby Dick*.

Engaged in a metaphysical search for the meaning of the voyage to the moon which NASA and the astronauts view as little more than a technological triumph, Mailer explores a wide range of subjects while centering interest on the relationship of technology to the human spirit and of both to God or Devil. He posits a tentatively held thesis that perhaps the death of romantic American heroism, symbolized by Hemingway's suicide and by his own attempts to fill the void Hemingway left, and its replacement with the hero-scientist

In the Center of History

who controls the machine for human advancement is America's true destiny as she carries God's vision to the stars. Not only does this thesis represent a significant change in Mailer's thinking about the American Wasp; it also provides justification for the enormous sums of money and the manpower expended on the space program while we continued to wage an anachronistic war and to condone domestic ills. It is not surprising that Mailer should be impressed with the power to change the shape of the future, but it comes as a surprise and a major disappointment to him that the dull and self-effacing Wasp instead of Mailer's army should lead the charge for God's forces into space, for it questions the efficacy of his methods. That the astronauts should be the new American heroes, the frontiersmen of outer space, is a blow to Ego, for the astronauts appeared to have none. The immensely powerful complex known as NASA impressed him as dull, humorless, and insidious. The language was functional—computerese—the machine the art. For Mailer all art was in communication while a machine which aided communication, like a typewriter, was only functional. The astronauts studiously avoided attaching more than a technological significance to their mission; they were self-effacing; they spoke in computerese; they did not fit at all Mailer's concept of heroes. His disappointment in Armstrong, Aldrin, and Collins is voiced in the following passage.

> . . . he could not forgive the astronauts their resolute avoidance of a heroic posture. It was somehow improper for a hero to be without flamboyance as if such modesty deprived his supporters of any large pleasure in his victories. What joy might be found in a world which would have no hope of a Hemingway? . . . it was as if the astronauts were there to demonstrate that heroism's previous relation to romance had been improper.
> The real heroism, he thought, was to understand, and because one understood, be even more full of fear at the enormity of what one understood, yet at that moment continue to be ready for the feat one had decided it was essential to perform.
> But the astronauts, brave men, proceeded on the paradoxical principle that fear once deposed by knowledge would make bravery redundant. It was in the complacent assumption that the universe was no majestic mansion of architectonics out there between evil and nobility, or strife on a darkling plain, but rather an ultimately

159

benign field of investigation which left Aquarius in the worst of his temper. (*Fire*, pp. 108–9)

What can men who speak like computers tell us of the moon? To deprive us of the wonder of the voyage is to deaden our souls a little more. Mailer's book is in this sense an antidote to the moon flight, redeeming it through the powerful art of language from the unbelievable dullness with which NASA had invested it. In so doing, Mailer reromanticizes the mission, elevating technology into a human triumph, conceiving it heroically as a "force which attempted to bring back answers from questions which had been considered to be without answers" (p. 125). In fact, Mailer goes so far as to liken Neil Armstrong's role to that of Ahab controlling the White Whale of a spaceship.

By the end of part one "Aquarius" (the persona Mailer adopts not only because it is his birth sign and symbolizes the end of one age and the seed of a new beginning but also because of the nature of the event and his inability to participate in it, which left him detached from his ego) has arrived at his hopeful thesis that the astronauts are the carriers of "God's vision of existence across the stars" (p. 150), for "it offered a reason why the heroes of our time were technologists, not poets, and the art was obliged to be in the exceptional engineering, while human communication had become the routine function" (p. 151).

Much of the remainder of *Of a Fire on the Moon*, divided into "Apollo" and "The Age of Aquarius," is composed of Mailer's research into statistical data and his personal encounters with NASA personnel and the astronauts. Since his participation is limited by the nature of the event, its mystery had to be explored through these other means. The book is heavily, perhaps overly, researched, and at times his application of the data seems highly fanciful, as when he interprets astrologically the preference of a large number of the astronauts for water sports. A more obvious factor, the climate of Houston, is overlooked. He is led to this extreme by his desire to probe the psychic rather than the scientific

160

nature of the event. One of the book's theses—and Mailer's claim to outdoing Freud—is that the dream is a "simulation chamber where the possible malfunctions of life tomorrow and life next year could be tested, where the alternate plans could be tried" (p. 159). The dream thus provides information for the familiar navigator of the subconscious through its "submersion into dread," and the navigator may then redesign his charts on the basis of this information. The theory is a progression beyond that concept of the navigator presented in earlier work and gives even greater meaning to the dream. The moonshot is then considered by analogy as "an exploration by the century itself into the possible consequences of its worship of technology, as if, indeed, the literal moon trip was a giant species of simulation to reveal some secret in the buried tendencies of our history" (p. 161).

Mailer's real concern in this book, and the one which most closely links him to Melville, is with the metaphysics of form. Forms are ambiguous as to their meaning. Mailer can delineate certain forms such as the spaceship and speculate about others such as the shape of God; but he cannot know their nature, for while some forms are designed to reveal meaning, such as Mailer's writing itself, others are deceptive, designed to conceal meaning. So the great question which Mailer returns to over and over in this book is whether in our explorations into space we act as unwitting agents of good or evil, or "whether the Space Program was the noblest expression of the Twentieth Century or the quintessential statement of our fundamental insanity" (p. 15). No final answer is possible, of course, but Mailer speculates that perhaps technology has intervened between man and God: "had the savage lived in a set of communions with the invisible messages of nature which we had pulverized with our amplifiers?" (p. 468). If so, then perhaps a return to divination by way of our senses, our instincts, our intuitions can restore the lost circuits of communication. At the book's conclusion, standing in front of a moon rock on display at the Manned Spacecraft Center in Houston, Mailer calls forth his "favorite saying, . . . trust the authority of your senses" to provide a tentative answer to the ambiguity of the moon-flight.

> . . . the expedition to the moon was finally a venture which might help to disclose the nature of the Lord and the Lucifer who warred for us; certainly the hour of happiness would be here when men who spoke like Shakespeare rode the ships: how many eons was that away! Yes, he had come to believe by the end of this long summer that probably we had to explore into outer space, for technology had penetrated the modern mind to such a depth that voyages in space might have become the last way to discover the metaphysical pits of that world of technique which choked the pores of modern consciousness—yes, we might have to go out into space until the mystery of new discovery would force us to regard the world once again as poets, behold it as savages who knew that if the universe was a lock, its key was metaphor rather than measure. (*Fire*, p. 471)

Perhaps Nick Carraway was wrong, for it seems that once again man is "face to face with something commensurate to his capacity for wonder." Mailer's philosophy of America's voyage to the moon is finally Edenic, religious, transcendent of technology, and very much a part of the mainstream of American literature. In *Of a Fire on the Moon* Mailer shows himself the descendant of a long line of American writers: Cooper, Hawthorne, James, Mencken, Lewis, and all who have criticized America's lack of a native culture, and one of a few to suggest that perhaps this very lack is a virtue in disguise. He writes

> Americans might yet run the world, they were certainly first on the way to the stars, and yet they had never filled the spaces between. Americans were still as raw as an unboiled potato [but] perhaps some instinct in American life had been working all these decades to keep the country innocent, keep it raw, keep it crude as a lout, have it indeed ready to govern the universe without an agreeable culture to call its own—for then, virgin ore, steadfastly undeveloped in all the hinterworld of the national psyche, a single idea could still electrify the land. (*Fire*, pp. 69–70)

Few Americans, it seems, were electrified for very long by manned spaceflight. Future Apollo moon landings were met with a casual indifference, very nearly a national boredom, for nothing is duller to Americans than a repeated spectacular. At present, funding for further space exploration has been drastically cut, for reasons as various as the enormous defense budget, a sagging economy, and a general incomprehension of the significance of man's explorations of his universe. If Mailer is right about the possibility of American electrification over a single idea, the shock will probably be of short duration. A generation dulled by a decade of crises such as the assassinations, the Vietnam War, Watergate, to name only the most obvious, is unlikely to be electrified by anything short of an invasion by aliens. Nonetheless, *Of a Fire on the Moon* raises questions of enormous significance, questions concerning the future directions of not only outer but of inner space exploration, with Mailer's heroics extended to attempts to bring the psychology of both men and machines under his control, an impossible task, yet one that needs to be undertaken if man is to control his own destiny.

As we have come to expect, Mailer selected as the subject of his next book another movement at the center of history, Women's Liberation. *The Prisoner of Sex* appeared in its entirety in the May 1971 issue of *Harper's*, for which the editor, Willie Morris, was fired. It seems that barriers against sexual explicitness and "obscene" language remain in the field of publishing, and that Mailer is still in the midst of gaining territory for his troops. The hardcover edition of *The Prisoner of Sex* followed in the fall of 1971.

In chapter one Mailer's first objective, as in *Of a Fire on the Moon*, is to establish his persona. His references to himself in the third person in these books and in *Miami* where he is "the reporter" differ from his treatment of himself in *The Armies of the Night* as "Mailer." In the latter, Mailer played all the roles, while in the succeeding three books he focused upon a single aspect of the self. Here Mailer refers to himself as the "PW," representing both Prisoner of Wedlock and Prizewinner, the "polar concepts to be regarded at opposite ends of his ego":[22] winner at writing and loser at love. The failure of Mailer's fourth marriage led him to play housewife and mother to his six children during the summer of 1970. The experience provided some perspective on the woman's need for liberation from the mindlessness which so often characterizes these roles. Mailer saw too that

> the themes of his life had gathered here. Revolution, tradition, sex and the homosexual, the orgasm, the family, the child and the political shape of the future, technology and human conception, waste and abortion, the ethics of the critic and the male mystique, black rights and new thoughts on women's rights. (*Prisoner*, p. 30)

His view of woman's role in promoting growth is called into question by the feminist movement. Consequently, the book centers around his defense of his early statement that "the prime responsibility of a woman probably is to be on earth long enough to find the best mate for herself, and conceive children who will improve the species" (p. 231). The search for that mate is not without courage, and Mailer concedes that women are not as free as they ought to be for the pursuit. And yet the direction in which radical feminism seems to be moving is toward freedom from their ultimate female identity: the ability to bear children. To Mailer the result of such "freedom" would imprison humanity. Since power is now technological, attempts by women to gain power must result in technologizing themselves—unless there is a primal urge to be masculine which women are fulfilling. With genetic engineering just around the corner, what is best and worth preserving about human life will be brought to judgment. Mailer has little confidence in the humanism of scientists and their choices of what are to be the enduring human characteristics. The following statement by a reputable philosopher illustrates the kind of thinking exhibited even by those concerned with moral improvement of the race.

> Our hope for the creation of a better world seems to lie in the harmonious integration of aspects of personality which are now frequently at odds with each other. If reason and emotion, intellect and feeling, the head and the heart and the hand, could be brought into synergic relations, we might unify personality and bring about what I have sometimes called cortico-thalamic integration. At present such characteristics as courage, imagination, love, and understanding are infrequent traits in exceptional individuals. These traits need to be integrated and universalized. We need to invent "mass production" techniques for evoking talents that are latent in mankind.[23]

In the Center of History

This statement suggests that large-scale genetic engineering can create those characteristics scientifically. To what end, one ought to ask, and who will decide which traits are desirable? If courage were a universal characteristic what would be its use?

Mailer's fear for the liberation of women from their wombs is not without justification. As a potential end of Women's Liberation it is antithetical to his belief that what is best about us is what we can create of ourselves that is good, whether it is a style, a book, a moment, or a new life.

Because his views on women are the subject of attack by feminists, in *The Prisoner of Sex* Mailer assumes the roles of defendent, lawyer, and judge in making his case against abdication of womanhood. The largest part of Mailer's case is the prosecution of Kate Millett's *Sexual Politics* and the defense of those attacked as misogynists by Millett: D. H. Lawrence, Henry Miller, Jean Genet, and himself. Unfortunately, Mailer has again allowed his opposition to dictate the form of his argument; his book depends upon the structure of hers. He is quite right, however, to attack her. Millett's singleminded presentation of her thesis results in sloppy or biased work; deliberate misreadings and quotations out of context abound, as Mailer points out. Lawrence and Miller were Mailer's antecedents on the subject of sex, and in defending them he defends his own view as well. Miller, he asserts, "has spent his literary life exploring the watershed of sex from that uncharted side which goes by the name of lust and it is an epic work for any man." Mailer defines lust as "that power to take over the ability to create and convert it to a force." It "exhibits all the attributes of junk" (*Prisoner*, pp. 109–10). Here Mailer draws a thematic line from Miller to Burroughs to himself. Mailer also is in accord with Miller's belief that "the eternal battle with woman sharpens our resistance, develops our strength, enlarges the scope of our cultural achievements," and that "the loss of sex polarity is part and parcel of the larger disintegration, the reflex of the soul's death and coincident with the disappearance of great men, great causes, great wars" (p. 125).

In Lawrence's thought Mailer finds two essential points to defend: one, that manhood is earned, not a birthright as proponents of Women's Liberation persist in believing; and two, that in good sex each partner brings his or her best to the act. Mailer continues to consider the orgasm as "the mirror to the character of the soul as the soul went over the hill into the next becoming" (p. 88).

In chapter four, "The Prisoner," Mailer defends his own work against Millett's attack. His basic premise is that a woman is in touch with the mysteries of creation through her womb, her link with the future, and that a man seeks to become a part of that mystery by planting his seed in her womb. It is precisely such awe of womanhood that feminists consider a carryover from the medieval veneration of Mary. Yet, Mailer points out, the alternative is to continue to move toward a "single permissive sexual standard" in which sex is exchanged like currency and in which ectogenesis will devoid the sexual act of any significance. The more meaning one attaches to sex the more one is its prisoner, the prisoner concludes. Finally, he says, let women be liberated from all but their wombs.

If Mailer is truly the archfoe of the liberation movement, it is because he insists on women's essential difference from men; a difference which he believes must be preserved if what we know as humanity is to continue to exist, for technology aims at universal sameness. By moving toward equality with men, he argues, women would destroy the uniqueness which is their strength. Although Mailer's existentialism pushes, through polarities, toward the synthesis which embraces all contradictions, he is unable to accept what he envisions as the end product of Women's Liberation, a masculinized, mechanized womanhood, not an androgynous society where male and female characteristics exist in harmony in each individual. Mailer has persisted in believing "that the spirit of the twentieth century was to convert man to a machine" (p. 29). Like *Of a Fire on the*

In the Center of History

Moon, The Prisoner of Sex explores the relationship between technology and humanism and here returns to the conservative position that the two are incompatible. Insisting that the roots of our humanism are in our past, in our lost instincts and dulled senses, Mailer goes so far as to posit that women may have already given up a subconscious power to accept or reject fertilization for the security of contraception. Neither does he believe, as most feminists and social scientists do, that sexual characteristics are a result of cultural conditioning. If Women's Liberation continues to gain momentum, perhaps it will enable us one day to learn whether there are any inherent differences between male and female other than the biological. But this is a question which Mailer has already answered to his satisfaction. In the language of his existentialism, he suggests, "the primary quality of man was an assertion, and on the consequence an isolation, that one had to alienate oneself from nature to become a man, . . . be perhaps directly opposed to nature, . . . if the calm of the seas is seen as the basic condition of nature, that man was a spirit of unrest who proceeded to become less masculine whenever he ceased to strive" (p. 132). Presumably, woman's primary quality, then, must be never to strive and never to oppose nature. We cannot grant Mailer such an assumption. Later in the book, however, when he allows that women should be as free as possible to find their most suitable mates, one infers that women may be masculine in the above sense as long as they maintain the sanctity of their wombs.

These arguments, which seem on the one hand to exclude women from existential growth and on the other insist that they ought to guard their sexual natures against technological invasion, seem contradictory and ill conceived. It is this that mars the substance of *The Prisoner of Sex*, although Mailer is particularly good in his role as attorney for the defense of Lawrence et al, and for the prosecution of Kate Millett. And his idea about the nature of masculinity would be intriguing if it were applied to women as well and called humanism.

167

Mailer's next book, *Existential Errands*, published in the spring of 1972, is a collection of essays written as long ago as 1963 but mostly after 1967. It is described by Mailer as "a miscellany of writings on existential themes."[24] Realizing that another five years had gone by without his producing the "big novel" promised since *Advertisements for Myself*, Mailer remarks in the preface to the collection that "it is a period when, with every thought of beginning a certain big novel which had been promised for a long time, the moot desire to have one's immediate say on contemporary matters kept diverting the novelistic impulse into journalism. Such passing books began to include many of the themes of the big novel."[25] It may well be that Mailer will have to venture very deeply into unknown territory—unknown to himself as well as to us—before he can outdo himself with the novel. The subjects of nearly all of his writing of the past six years are fixed events which, with the exception of the Pentagon march, Mailer could alter only in their meaning, not in their form. His existential vision having governed his interpretations of these events, his style therefore becomes all of his form, all of his new creation. The novel, as he sees it, should engage all of his talents more deeply than his recent writing; yet having established himself as the "Interpreter of Nuance in Contemporary Events," he cannot seem to give up the role to write the novel. Ironically, in the *The Prisoner of Sex* Mailer had remarked that

> If there had been a period when he believed completely in the tonic overhauling of the state and had written his prose with fingers trembling with anger at the Establishment, he had by now lost that essential belief in himself which was critical to the idea that one could improve the world (and knew he might not regain that belief until he had written the novel of his life and succeeded in passing judgement on himself—if indeed one could). (P. 56)

I argued earlier that a book like *The Armies of the Night*, which seems to have the most potential to alter the American consciousness, was more significant in terms of Mailer's early ambition than a novel like *Why Are We in Vietnam?*, which from all indications failed to communicate with its intended audience. And yet *The Armies of the*

Night's virtue, Mailer as visible hero actively seeking to change history, has not carried over to the books which have followed. The risks he is taking in his writing have diminished, although the greatest risk of all—his reputation—is at stake with each publication.

It is a dilemma which Mailer faces in pursuing his goal of the alteration of the contemporary consciousness, for he sees its potential in events of the day to which millions are exposed through the electronic and printed media, yet he reveres the novel as the highest form of writing and has bought his "plots of time" to work on it by accepting short, high-paying assignments which further delay its appearance. For personal reasons he must maintain a level of income attainable, until recently, only through this type of writing, a fact of life which he and we who wish to see him write the novel of his life have lived with. This is not to say that such work is not valuable; rather, it causes one to question whether Mailer wishes to or indeed can continue to live by the aesthetic which requires him to grow into more and avoid the traps of success and self-parody for which he castigated Hemingway and Faulkner. In 1974 Mailer received a million-dollar contract from Little, Brown for "a novel large in scope,"[26] to be five to seven hundred thousand words in length and to take from five to seven years to write and which may break down into several novels. This insures him a steady income to work on the novel if he can turn his full attention to it.

A book such as *Existential Errands*, a miscellany of reprints on no very cohesive theme, does little to enhance Mailer's reputation. He does attempt to group the material, although not as coherently as in his previous three collections, *Advertisements for Myself*, *Presidential Papers*, and *Cannibals and Christians*, all of which included editorializing after the fact on Mailer's part.

The collection is divided into three parts. Part one, "Clues to the Aesthetics of the Arena," includes essays on boxing, bullfighting, theatre, and film, all discussed elsewhere in this book with the exception of "King of the Hill" (originally published in *Life* as "Ego" and issued as a separate paper-back with the title "*King of the Hill*").[27] Like his earlier piece, "Death," on the Patterson-Liston fight in *Presidential Papers*, "King of the Hill" deals with the metaphysics of a championship fight, this time the Ali-Frazier match. Obsessed as always with the ambiguities of form, of the drives of outstanding men, Mailer cannot decide whether Muhammad Ali is "a demon or a saint" and metaphorizes him as "the swiftest embodiment of human intelligence we have had yet" and as "the very spirit of the twentieth century" (*Existential Errands*, p. 4).

Whatever the significance of the fight, we have come to expect that Mailer see all of his subjects in terms of these metaphors, making his writing seem formulaic, predictable in substance if not in style. We are prepared to accept the possibility that the apocalypse may reside in such events as space flights or political conventions, but it is difficult to accept this in a boxing match, albeit a championship fight. Whether or not Ali is good or evil seems of minor significance compared to the morality of a presidential candidate, and Mailer's application of his metaphors to situations and individuals of unequal dimensions tends to deflate them all, which is the price he pays for a coherent philosophy.

At any rate, Mailer's interest in boxing, like bullfighting, is long standing and definitive of the existential confrontation at the heart of his aesthetics. It is also Hemingway-esque. Among his closest friends are a number of ex-prizefighters. Presently Mailer has two more fight books in the works, one a full-length account of the October 1974 Ali-Foreman fight in Zaire, to be published in two parts in the May and June 1975 issues of *Playboy* and as a separate book, and the other a collection of all of his fight pieces including the new one.

The remainder of *Existential Errands* is divided into "Hints to the Aesthetic of the Study," mainly short pieces too diverse to categorize, and "Grips on the Aesthetic of the Street," including writing on "Black Power" and "White Politics," generally extentions of his theories of violence

In the Center of History

and left-conservatism discussed earlier. While not a particularly satisfying book in itself, it is good to have at hand such items as Mailer's National Book Award acceptance speech and his one-act play, "A Fragment from Vietnam."

With Mailer's next book, *St. George and the Godfather*, we move back into the arena of politics and apocalypse. Rushed into print in paperback only less than two months before the 1972 presidential election, the book was designed, as were its predecessors, to influence the election's outcome. Mailer offers himself as the medium whose message we can trust, thereby rescuing our dulled brains from the effects of the electronic media. "The fundamental message of television," Mailer contends, "is an electronic drone of oscillating dots" which produce an "all-but-unperceived nausea" so that "the art of television is to find a content which can sit agreeably with the nausea," a feat which the Republican convention accomplished by its resemblance to a professionally produced spectacular.[28] One can infer from his analysis of the conventions as media that Mailer offers his own perceptions as an antidote to TV nausea, in addition to his usual role as navigator and interpreter of the events. His method is disclosed in an unusually short statement which assumes on the reader's part a knowledge of his Aquarian persona and of his reportorial techniques:

> ... Norman Mailer, who looked to rule himself by Voltaire's catch-all percept, "Once a philosopher, twice a pervert" and preferred therefore never to repeat a technique, was still obliged to call himself Aquarius again for he had not been in Miami two days before he knew he would not write objectively about the Convention of '72. There were too many questions, and (given the probability of a McGovern steam roller) not enough drama to supply answers. He would be obliged to drift through events, and use the reactions of his brain for evidence. A slow brain, a muddy river, and therefore no name better suited to himself again than the modest and half-invisible Aquarius. Enough of Ego Liberation. (*St. George*, p. 3)

St. George and the Godfather is a more modest book than *Miami and the Siege of Chicago*, more subdued, less colorful both because of the nature of the events and the mood of the author. Unlike the conventions of 1968, where Mailer saw

171

America at war with itself in the streets of Chicago, or some drama even in the feeble attempts to block Nixon's nomination, the 1972 conventions were decidedly undramatic. Mailer's preferred aesthetic is the dialectic; he found none here. His free-floating ego found no drama of disproportions to attach itself to, and consequently the book suffers from the author's depression over the middling proportions of the two parties' candidates. McGovern he sees as principled but unexciting, Nixon dull but possibly unprincipled, and Mailer, given the set of metaphors he is committed to, must conclude that "the nature of the undramatic Satan, true evil one, was to conceal himself, after all" (p. 23).

If the limitation of the Democrats and their candidate is that they are insufficiently evil, the Republicans' choice is the "grandmaster" of the mediocre, what Mailer now calls the "wad" of middle-class Wasps committed to Nixon, whom he condemns because "the gleam in their eye speaks of no desire to go beyond the spirit they have already been given" (p. 200). These are the patriots whose "failure to recognize that total faith in one's country might be as dangerous as total faith in one's own moral worth, even worse, for total faith in one's country might be as dangerous as total patriotism, one's own soul was no longer there to be lost" (p. 208). Believing that the country itself is America's religion and the political parties its "true churches," Mailer sees what he considers the essential difference between the congregations of the two candidates. If McGovern's church was composed of the newly confirmed, eager to become the saviors of all men, Nixon's was made up of the elect, secure in the knowledge of their righteousness and salvation, to whom only American blood is a sacrament. Attitudes toward Vietnam constitute the only battleground between the parties that Mailer finds morally significant. Although a sizeable issue, it does not result in "the major confrontation for which he looked" (p. 221) during his weeks in Miami Beach. In a revealing passage, Mailer becomes "almost nostalgic" over the "good wars" he has missed (p. 225), wars in which there was a camaraderie among men with a common

In the Center of History

enemy, and the good life was to be a war correspondent involved in an action which is not "sad and absurd and pointless and lost" like the symbolic wars he watches in the streets (p. 226). This passage attests that three of the most powerful influences on Mailer's scheme of things have been war and Ernest Hemingway and the intersection of the two. Watching the demonstrators in Flamingo Park from his hotel window, Mailer no longer identifies with them, observing that "when the time came for the real war, if it ever came to America, he would presumably be enough of a man to recognize it" (p. 168). He has, then, "turned some corner in his life" (ibid.) not yet reached five years earlier in Washington or even four years before in Chicago. He is sensing here that symbolic wars are as futile as writing about them. Some loss of faith in his own powers as a writer and dialectician accompanies his observations of the lumbering machinations of the political system, some sensing of impotence in a hint of the massiveness of the defeat of McGovern, insufficiently evil to combat his opponent, so never really becoming Saint George. And beyond suggesting Nixon's resemblance to a Mafia *don capo* (with as yet no hint of the Watergate scandal) to whom murder is justifiable outside of the family, the writer can do nothing to impede the landslide reelection of the president.

Consequently, the book ends on a note of depression which somehow rings truer than those which intimate that decisive battles lie ahead. Mailer seems to be becoming more conscious that the ambiguities he discerns are locked in their forms, and that not even his metaphors can disengage them and produce the Armageddon he awaits.

The book is somewhat interesting in its particulars. Mailer is still master of incisive portraits of the American character, here represented in her politicians, and sensitive to portents of power. We are treated to this description of Hubert Humphrey, making his last futile attempt at the presidency:

> Time had glued him together with less than her usual address. Humphrey looked like a man whose features had been repaired after

an accident; if the collar slipped, the welts would show. It was the horror of his career that as he came to the end of it, his constituency was real (if antipathetic to one another—what did his Blacks, old and middle-aged Jews, and trade unions have to do with one another?) but he was not real, not nearly so real as the constituency, more like some shattered, glued, and jolly work of art, a Renaissance priest of the Vatican who could not even cross a marble floor without pieties issuing from his skirt. Father Hubert. He had the look of a man who knew where the best wine was kept, but old age would have to conquer his desire to lisp when dogma was invoked. (*St. George*, pp. 18–19)

and this nugget on Lawrence O'Brien's finesse as Democratic convention chairman: "He seemed born with the ability to walk through a barnyard on his way to the cotillion and never have to wipe his pumps" (p. 42).

Interviews with McGovern, McCarthy, Eagleton, and Kissinger provide confrontations over which Mailer can exert some control. That with Henry Kissinger, a man with a palpable charisma, is fascinating but dissatisfying to Mailer because "one did not get messages from his presence of good or evil, rather of intelligence, and the warm courtesy of Establishment" (p. 120), while a meeting with Senator Eagleton produces the comment that "no matter how many times it happened, it was unnerving to meet men who had been near to high office and recognize they were no more magnificent than yourself" (p. 100).

On the whole, *St. George and the Godfather* is a worthy supplement and even a necessary alternative to the news media's convention reportage. Yet, although in it Mailer appears to have retreated slightly from the visionary toward the realistic mode (or, as Northrop Frye would put it, from the romantic to the ironic), the book's contribution to American letters is slighter than that of *The Armies of the Night* or *Of a Fire on the Moon*, which push more deeply into unknown territory, and it is dated in a way the others are not.

In July of 1973 Mailer's much-anticipated biography of Marilyn Monroe appeared. Early reviews would have it that Mailer had sacrificed his talent to his bank account, for the book brought him a sizeable advance, along with subsidiary rights and 50 percent of the royalties, while the twenty-four photographers who contributed 100 photographs of Monroe would split the rest. Pauline Kael in a page-one review in the *New York Times Book Review* called the book a "rip-off with genius."[29] Mailer responded to these charges in an interview:

> . . . why does a writer not have the same right to make money that a capitalist does, or an entrepreneur or a corporation? [Rick Stratton asks, "You said, once you've decided that you are going to do a book for money, then you have to get into the existentialism of the act, which is whether you do it well or you do it badly, whether the book will finally make you deader as a writer or more alive." Mailer responds,] If you're doing something for money, the only way you can get through it alive is to give more than was requested. . . . If you sit down and you say, there is such a thing as a literary gift and God gave me one, and I'm now using it to earn a living, then the only absolution is to fall in love with the object of my fee. Which is what I'm saying I did.[30]

Controversy also sprang up over Mailer's heavy reliance on former biographies of Monroe, and Mailer was sued for plagiarism (surely the most insulting accusation he has met) for not paying enough in permissions to one of these biographers, although he scrupulously acknowledged all sources. Too, Mike Wallace in an unfairly edited interview with Mailer on "Sixty Minutes" challenged Mailer's tenuously held theory that the CIA and FBI may have arranged Monroe's murder to embarrass the Kennedy family and give credence to the hypothetical affair between Monroe and Robert F. Kennedy by making it look as if she had committed suicide over Kennedy's unrequited love.[31] Kael and others also attacked Mailer's portrait of Arthur Miller, whom he saw as the victim of Marilyn's lack of identity, unable, as were her first two husbands, to provide Marilyn with the ego she needed, despite his efforts. Miller is described as at an impasse in his writing, and Mailer attributes to him the motive to marry Monroe in order to revitalize an impoverished imagination. As is true of most of Mailer's contribution to Monroe lore, this is pure speculation which Mailer's novelistic imagination tells him approaches the truth not discernible through plain fact. He describes his method early in the book.

It is possible there is no instrument more ready to capture the elusive quality of Monroe's nature than a novel. Set a thief to catch a thief, and put an artist on an artist. Could the solution be nothing less vainglorious than a novel of Marilyn Monroe? Written in the form of biography? Since it would rely in the main on other sources, it could hardly be more than a long biographical article—nonetheless, a *species* of novel ready to play by the rules of biography. No items could be made up and evidence would be provided when facts were moot. Yet he would never delude himself that he might be telling a story which could possibly be more accurate than a fiction since he would often be quick to imagine the interior of many a closed and silent life, and with the sanction of a novelist was going to look into the unspoken impulses of some of his real characters. At the end, if successful, he would have offered a literary hypothesis of a *possible* Marilyn Monroe who might actually have lived and fit most of the facts available. If his instincts were good, then future facts discovered about her would not have to war with the character he created. A reasonable venture! It satisfied his fundamental idea that acquisition of knowledge for a literary man was best achieved in those imaginative acts of appropriation picked up by the disciplined exercise of one's skill.[32]

This "novel biography," what one might expect of Mailer's first encounter with a new genre, is a spinoff from the preceding novel histories. The essential difference between *Marilyn* and another heavily researched book like *Of a Fire on the Moon* lies almost entirely in the subject, for the methods of each are similar. Of course, Mailer never knew Monroe, but he could interview some who did, could spend weeks viewing twenty-four of her thirty films, reading other biographies of her. That his perceptions of her were obtained secondhand need not diminish his accomplishment. Those who criticized Mailer's heavy reliance on the fact gatherings of other Monroe biographers did not complain of his not having initiated the Apollo 11 flight or the political conventions; once again we have Mailer interpreting facts for us, not creating them, and dispelling where possible "factoids . . . facts which have no existence before appearing in a magazine or newspaper, creations which are not so much lies as a product to manipulate emotion in the Silent Majority" (*Marilyn*, p. 18). Plagiarism charges obscured the research Mailer did do for the book as well as his scrupulous documentation of sources.[33]

176

In the Center of History

His approach that of a "psychohistorian," Mailer works through intuitions which he receives from Monroe's acting, comparing them with the known facts of her life. What interested him in her, not unexpectedly, was the ambiguity of her nature: frigid and sensual, ambitious and submissive, the contradictions in her character became the focus of Mailer's writing. He determines that she had talent but not identity, that her lack of one led her to borrow identities from the roles she played. Her identity crisis by extension becomes the crisis of the American culture, whose Faustian ambitions clash with its lack of roots in the past. Her apparent lack of insight into her own nature, her suicide which on a subconscious level enabled her to pass on what was left of her soul, these things fascinate Mailer and the reader as we follow where his mind carries us.

We have encountered Mailer's conception of Monroe as the mythic American before. As Stephen Rojack was about to leave America on the last page of *An American Dream*, he places a psychic phone call to Cherry who tells him, "Marilyn says to say hello. We get along, which is odd, you know, because girls don't swing." Marilyn is, of course, Cherry's archetype: the small town girl from the American school of hard knocks, elevated to princess by the men who adore her freshness and the quality of innocence she conveys despite the corruption she has lived amidst. Marilyn, then and now, represented to Mailer the desire of America to create itself anew but also its schizophrenic division from its deepest memories, its connections with its past. Through the medium of film (represented by the book's rich photography), Mailer believes, and the actor's struggle to make a lie the truth, the identity crisis displays its aesthetics, which we identify as Mailer's own. Ironically, the sheer effort of creation may expend the self's resources, which must be made of sterner stuff than Monroe's in order to survive.

In Mailer's view, "Monroe had a huge ego considering how void she felt of identity," ego being defined as "awareness of one's will. Knowing at a given moment what you want to do."[34] But finally her ego was insufficient, unless in fact she did commit suicide intentionally in order to save her soul.

One of the reasons why Mailer finds Monroe fascinating, I think, is that they have this in common: both are quick-change artists with multiple personas rather than a single well-developed identity and with a strong sense of their own wills. Hemingway was also this kind of existential artist, who "was forging his identity every day of his life."[35]

The identity Mailer assumed in his next piece, *The Faith of Graffiti*, was that of "Aesthetic Investigator" (or "A-I") in order to further explore this question of identity and ego and their interrelationships in the pop art phenomenon, graffiti: not the rest room wall variety combining obscenity, iconoclasm, and punning, but the naming of oneself and then "getting the name around" in spray-paint calligraphy. *The Faith of Graffiti* is primarily a book of photographs for which Mailer wrote the accompanying essay and is not of enough length or significance to concern us further here, except for what it indicates of his current interests. He finds graffiti, in its assertion of ego against totalitarianism and in its aesthetic, symptomatic of our national disease: schizophrenia.

> The city [New York] would finally tolerate . . . every petty crime of the street, and every major pollution, but it could not accept a towering rain forest of graffiti on all the forty-story walls. Yes, build a wall and balance a disease. For the blank wall of the new architecture was the deadening agent to balance the growing violence beneath. (*The Faith of Graffiti* [unpaginated])

The subject obviously brings together a number of Mailer's continued themes, which is why he agreed to do the piece. *The Faith of Graffiti* also contains the seed of a theme which I believe him to be exploring in his new novel; he postulates that graffiti is "our first art of Karma," for "If our name is enormous to us, it is also not real—as if we have come from other places than the name, and lived in other lives." In a recent interview with me Mailer reveals that he was introduced to the subject of karma by James Jones in about 1953 and that in the last three or four years he has come to believe that Jones was right, that karma makes sense.[36] It is a subject he believes more appropriate for a novel than an essay, and, as it seems to be in the forefront of his thoughts these days, it is a likely subject for the new novel. To date (early 1975), Mailer has completed 120,000 words of the novel, of which 100,000 were submitted to Little, Brown in August 1974 to be published either as a separate novel or as the first volume of a large work. While Mailer is reluctant, as ever, to talk about a work in progress, he did indicate that some early scenes take place in Egypt, and that the book deals with past, present, and future time.[37] Those who have read this material have described it as epic, Jungian, Tolstoian, dealing with a racial theme. In short, it looks as if it will be what Mailer has been promising us and himself for so long.

When not working on the novel, Mailer is pursuing his interests through more of the new journalistic writing. The work on the Ali-Foreman fight, for example, originally to be a short piece, went 40,000 words before coming to the fight itself. The first part is concerned with the geographical and cultural contexts of Africa, in which the fight took place. Mailer's engagement with the Dark Continent should be a most interesting subject and should suggest further parallels with modern writers, especially Hemingway. A collection of his pieces on boxing, that symbolic existential battleground, including excerpts from this new book, will be published later this year.

So his work goes on, with explorations into unknown territories of subject and style refining while reaffirming his existential beliefs. The more he writes the more difficult it becomes to see each new piece as a work in its own right and instead to see it as a part of the progress or regression of a rather spectacular literary career. The greater the artist's ambition, the more vulnerable he is to attack; the more he accomplishes, the more we expect of him.

Had Mailer not determined himself a quarter of a century ago the leading contender for the Hemingway-Faulkner title, or been accepted at last by many as the heavyweight champ, we should find objectivity towards his work easier to come by. To take him seriously requires an engagement not only with his ideas and his style, which may well constitute a series of blows to the head and the vitals, but also with his public personality, for it is to know them as inseparable, however inconveniently this complicates our assessment of him. And by placing himself in contention for the title of our most significant living writer he has made the stakes of his success dangerously high. If his new novel isn't at least as good as *Remembrance of Things Past* or as monumental as *War and Peace*, we will have grounds for a technical knockout. Of course, he has been laying his big novel before us all along: its subject matter the territory he has regained from the totalitarians for the humanists, and its style the creation of himself. In time we will learn his value to us, if we become existentialists too.

NOTES

1. Mailer, quoted in an interview with James Toback, in Toback's article "At Play in the Fields of the Bored," p. 154.
2. Manso, *Running against the Machine*, p. xii.
3. Ibid., pp. 12-14.
4. Ibid., pp. 3-4.
5. Ibid., p. 138.
6. See Flaherty's account of the campaign in *Managing Mailer*.
7. J. Anthony Lukas, "Norman Mailer Enlists His Private Army to Act in Film," p. 41.
8. J. Anthony Lukas, "Mailer Film Party a Real Bash: 1 Broken Jaw, 2 Bloody Heads," p. 29.
9. John M. Lee, "Mailer, in London, Trades Jabs with Audience over New Film," p. 21.
10. Norman Mailer, *Maidstone: A Mystery*, p. 47. All further references are cited in the text, and the title will be shortened to *Maidstone*.
11. It is unlikely that Mailer will make more films unless he receives funding. His personal investment of $350,000 in *Maidstone* was largely irrecoverable.
12. Norman Mailer, "A Transit to Narcissus," pp. 3-10. Interestingly, this is the title of a youthful, unpublished Mailer novel.
13. John O. Stark, "Norman Mailer's Works from 1963 to 1968," p. 184.

In the Center of History

14. Norman Mailer, *The Faith of Graffiti* (unpaginated). All further references are cited in the text, and the title will be shortened to *Graffiti*.
15. Laura Adams, "Existential Aesthetics: An Interview with Norman Mailer," p. 209.
16. Richard Poirier, "Mailer: Good Form and Bad," p. 46 (reprinted in Laura Adams, ed., *Will the Real Norman Mailer Please Stand Up?*).
17. At Ohio State University, October 27, 1972; University of Dayton, March 6, 1973; and Wright State University, October 28, 1973.
18. Accounts of the party appeared as follows: John Leonard, "The Last Word," p. 35; "A Half Century of Mailer," *Newsweek*, February 19, 1973, p. 78; Patricia Bosworth, "Fifth Estate at the Four Seasons," pp. 5-7.
19. Norman Mailer, "The Guest Word," pp. 55 and 46.
20. Norman Mailer, *Miami and the Siege of Chicago*, pp. 12 and 14. All further references are cited in the text, and the title will be shortened to *Miami*.
21. Stark, "Norman Mailer's Work," p. 167.
22. Norman Mailer, *The Prisoner of Sex*, p. 9. All further references are cited in the text, and the title will be shortened to *Prisoner*.
23. Oliver L. Reiser, "Our World in Revolution," p. 49.
24. Norman Mailer, *Existential Errands*, p. ix.
25. Ibid.
26. Adams, "Existential Aesthetics," p. 210.
27. Norman Mailer, "Ego," pp. 18f, 19, 22-30, 32, and 36; and "*King of the Hill*," p. 25.
28. Norman Mailer, *St. George and the Godfather*, pp. 176-79. All further references are cited in the text, and the title will be shortened to *St. George*.
29. Pauline Kael, review of *Marilyn*, pp. 1-3.
30. Richard Stratton, "The Rolling Stone Interview, Part I," p. 42.
31. CBS, July 13, 1973.
32. Norman Mailer, *Marilyn*, p. 20. All further references are to this text.
33. There is no question of Mailer's stealing another writer's work involved in the charges. He simply quoted more passages than his publishers paid for in the original permissions. Mailer countersued Zolotow for defamation of character; Zolotow subsequently apologized to Mailer, a fact which received little publicity, and both suits were dropped.
34. Adams, "Existential Aesthetics," p. 213.
35. Ibid.
36. Ibid., p. 207.
37. Richard Stratton, "The Rolling Stone Interview Part II," p. 45.

BIBLIOGRAPHY

Note: Primary Sources is a list in chronological order of Mailer's works through 1974. The date of original publication of each work is included in brackets following its title.

Primary Sources

Books and Films

The Naked and the Dead. [1948] Toronto: New American Library of Canada, 1969.

Barbary Shore. [1951] New York: New American Library, n.d.

The Deer Park (novel). [1955] New York: Berkley Medallion Books, 1969.

The White Negro. [1957] San Francisco: City Lights Book Shop, 1957.

Advertisements for Myself. [1959] New York: Berkley Medallion Books, 1969.

Deaths for the Ladies (and other disasters). [1962] New York: New American Library, 1971.

The Presidential Papers. [1963] Harmondsworth, Middlesex, England: Penguin Books, 1968.

An American Dream. [*Esquire*, January to August, 1964, revised 1965] New York: Dell, 1966.

Cannibals and Christians. [1966] New York: Dell, 1970.

The Deer Park (play). [1967] New York: Dial Press, 1967.

The Bullfight: A Photographic Narrative with Text by Norman Mailer. [1967] New York: CBS Legacy Collection Book, distributed by Macmillan, 1967.

The Short Fiction of Norman Mailer. [1967] New York: Dell, 1967.

Wild 90 (film). [1967] New York: Supreme Mix, 1967.

Why Are We in Vietnam?. [1967] New York: Berkley Medallion Books, 1968.

The Idol and the Octopus. [1968] New York: Dell, 1968.

Beyond the Law (film). [1968] New York: Supreme Mix, 1968.

The Armies of the Night: History as a Novel/the Novel as History. [1968] Toronto: New American Library of Canada, 1968.

Bibliography

Miami and the Siege of Chicago: An Informal History of the Republican and Democratic Conventions of 1968. [1968] New York: New American Library, 1968.

Maidstone (film). [1968] New York: Supreme Mix, 1969.

Of a Fire on the Moon. [1970] New York: Little, Brown, 1970.

"King of the Hill". [1971] New York: New American Library, 1971.

The Prisoner of Sex. [1971] New York: Little, Brown, 1971.

Maidstone: A Mystery. [1971] New York: New American Library, 1971.

Existential Errands. [1971] Boston: Little, Brown, 1972.

St. George and the Godfather. [1972] New York: New American Library, 1972.

Marilyn. [1973] New York: Grosset & Dunlap, 1973.

The Faith of Graffiti. [1974] New York: Praeger Publishers, 1974.

Articles

"The Big Bite," *Esquire*, December 1963, p. 26.

"Some Dirt in the Talk: A Candid History of an Existential Movie Called *Wild 90*." *Esquire*, December 19, 1967, pp. 190–94, 261, 264–69.

"The Crazy One." *Playboy*, October 1967, pp. 91–92, 112, 211–14.

"Up the Family Tree." *Partisan Review* 35 (Spring 1968): 234–52.

"Ego." *Life*, March 19, 1971, pp. 18f, 19, 22–30, 32, 36.

"The Guest Word." *New York Times Book Review*, March 11, 1973, p. 55.

"A Transit to Narcissus" [review of *Last Tango in Paris*]. *New York Review of Books*, May 17, 1973, pp. 3–10.

Secondary Sources

Adams, Laura. "Criticism of Norman Mailer: A Selected Checklist." *Modern Fiction Studies* 17 (Autumn, 1971): 455–63.

———, ed. *Will the Real Norman Mailer Please Stand Up?* Port Washington, New York: Kennikat Press, 1974.

———. *Norman Mailer: A Comprehensive Bibliography.* Metuchen, New Jersey: Scarecrow Press, 1974.

———. "Existential Aesthetics: An Interview with Norman Mailer." *Partisan Review* 42 (1975), 197–214.

Aldridge, John W. *After the Lost Generation.* New York: Noonday Press, 1958, pp. 133–41, *et passim*.

———. "From Vietnam to Obscenity." *Harper's*, February 1968, pp. 91–92, 94–97.

Berthoff, Warner. "Witness and Testament: Two Contemporary Classics." In *Aspects of Narrative*, edited by J. Hillis Miller. New York: Columbia University Press, 1971.

Bone, Robert A. "Private Mailer Re-enlists." *Dissent* 7 (Autumn 1960): 389–94.

Booth, Wayne C. *The Rhetoric of Fiction.* Chicago: University of Chicago Press, 1967.

184

Bibliography

Bosworth, Patricia. "Fifth Estate at the Four Seasons." *Saturday Review of the Arts*, March 1973, pp. 5-7.

Braudy, Leo. "Norman Mailer: The Pride of Vulnerability." In *Norman Mailer: A Collection of Critical Essays*, edited by Leo Braudy. Englewood, New Jersey: Prentice-Hall, 1972, pp. 1-20.

Breslow, Paul. "The Hipster and the Radical." *Studies on the Left* 1 (Spring, 1960): 102-5.

Carroll, Paul. "*Playboy* Interview: Norman Mailer." *Playboy*, January 1968, pp. 69-72, 74, 76, 78, 80, 82-84.

Chase, Richard. *The American Novel and its Tradition*. Garden City: Doubleday, 1957.

Cirlot, J. E. *A Dictionary of Symbols*. New York: Philosophical Library, 1962.

Corrington, John William. "An American Dreamer." *Chicago Review* 18 (1965): 58-66.

Cowan, Michael. "The Americanness of Norman Mailer." In *Norman Mailer: A Collection of Critical Essays*, edited by Leo Braudy. Englewood Cliffs, New Jersey: Prentice-Hall, 1972. Reprinted in Laura Adams, ed. *Will the Real Norman Mailer Please Stand Up?*

Dupee, F. W. "The American Norman Mailer." *Commentary*, February 1960, pp. 128-32.

Ellison, Jane. "Cancer, Personality Linked, Psychologist Says." *Dayton Daily News*, April 16, 1971, p. 1.

Fiedler, Leslie A. *Love and Death in the American Novel*. Rev. ed. New York: Dell, 1966.

Flaherty, Joe. *Managing Mailer*. New York: Coward-McCann, 1969.

Foster, Richard. *Norman Mailer*. Minneapolis: University of Minnesota Press, 1968.

———. "Mailer and the Fitzgerald Tradition." In *Norman Mailer: A Collection of Critical Essays*, edited by Leo Braudy. Englewood Cliffs, New Jersey: Prentice-Hall, 1972.

Frye, Northrop. *Anatomy of Criticism*. New York: Atheneum, 1968.

Fuller, Edmund. *Man in Modern Fiction: Some Minority Opinions on Contemporary American Writing*. New York: Random House, 1958.

Gilman, Richard. "Why Mailer Wants to be President." *New Republic*, February 8, 1964, pp. 17-20, 22-24.

Gutman, Stanley T. "Mankind in Barbary: The Individual and Society in the Novels of Norman Mailer." Ph.D. dissertation, Duke University, 1971.

"A Half Century of Mailer." *Newsweek*, February 19, 1973, p. 78.

Hampshire, Stuart. "Mailer United." *New Statesman*, October 13, 1961, pp. 515-16.

Harper, Howard M., Jr. *Desperate Faith: A Study of Bellow, Salinger, Mailer, Baldwin and Updike*. Chapel Hill: University of North Carolina Press, 1967.

Hassan, Ihab. *Radical Innocence: Studies in the Contemporary American Novel*. New York: Harper & Row, 1961.

Hux, Samuel Holland. "American Myth and Existential Vision: The In-

Bibliography

digenous Existentialism of Mailer, Bellow, Styron, and Ellison." Ph.D. dissertation, University of Connecticut, 1965.

Kael, Pauline. Review of *Marilyn. New York Times Book Review*, July 1973, pp. 1–3.

Kaufmann, Donald L. *Norman Mailer: The Countdown/The First Twenty Years.* Carbondale: Southern Illinois University Press, 1969.

———. "The Long Happy Life of Norman Mailer." *Modern Fiction Studies* 17 (Autumn, 1971): 347–59.

Lawler, Robert W. "Norman Mailer: The Connection of New Circuits." Ph.D. dissertation, Claremont Graduate School, 1969.

Lawrence, D. H. *Studies in Classic American Literature.* New York: Viking Press, 1964.

Lee, John M. "Mailer, in London, Trades Jabs with Audience Over New Film." *New York Times,* October 17, 1970, p. 21.

Leeds, Barry H. *The Structured Vision of Norman Mailer.* New York: New York University Press, 1969.

Lelchuk, Alan. *American Mischief.* New York: Farrar, Straus and Giroux, 1973.

Leonard, John. "The Last Word." *New York Times Book Review,* February 18, 1973, p. 35.

Lewis, R. W. B. *The American Adam: Innocence, Tragedy and Tradition in the Nineteenth Century.* Chicago: University of Chicago Press, 1965.

Lukas, J. Anthony. "Norman Mailer Enlists His Private Army to Act in Film." *New York Times,* July 23, 1968, p. 41.

———. "Mailer Film Party a Real Bash: 1 Broken Jaw, 2 Bloody Heads." *New York Times,* July 31, 1968, p. 29.

Manso, Peter, ed. *Running Against the Machine.* Garden City, N.Y.: Doubleday, 1969.

Marx, Leo. *The Machine in the Garden: Technology and the Pastoral Ideal in America.* New York: Oxford University Press, 1967.

McLuhan, Marshall. *Understanding Media: The Extensions of Man.* New York: New American Library, 1964.

Mudrick, Marvin. "Mailer and Styron: Guests of the Establishment." *Hudson Review* 17 (Autumn 1964): 346–66.

Muste, John M. "Norman Mailer and John Dos Passos: The Question of Influence." *Modern Fiction Studies* 17 (Autumn 1971): 361–74.

Podhoretz, Norman. "Norman Mailer: The Embattled Vision." In *Recent American Fiction,* edited by Joseph J. Waldmeir. Boston: Houghton Mifflin, 1963.

Poirier, Richard. *A World Elsewhere: The Place of Style in American Literature.* New York: Oxford University Press, 1966.

———. *The Performing Self.* New York: Oxford University Press, 1971.

———. *Norman Mailer.* Modern Masters Series. New York: Viking Press, 1972.

———. "Mailer: Good Form and Bad," *Saturday Review,* April 22, 1972, pp. 42–46. Reprinted in Laura Adams, ed. *Will the Real Norman Mailer Please Stand Up?*

Reich, Charles. *The Greening of America.* New York: Bantam Books, 1970.

Bibliography

Reiser, Oliver L. "Our World in Revolution." In *Social Speculations: Visions for Our Time*, edited by Richard Kostelanetz. New York: William Morrow, 1971.

Rideout, Walter B. *The Radical Novel in the United States: 1900-1954.* Cambridge: Harvard University Press, 1956.

Samuels, Charles T. "The Novel, USA: Mailerrhea." *Nation* 205 (October 23, 1967): 405-6.

Schulz, Max F. *Radical Sophistication: Studies in Contemporary Jewish-American Novelists.* Athens: Ohio University Press, 1969.

Stark, John O. "Norman Mailer's Work from 1963 to 1968." Ph.D. dissertation, University of Wisconsin, 1970.

———. "*Barbary Shore*: The Basis of Mailer's Best Work," *Modern Fiction Studies* 17 (Autumn 1971): 403-8.

Stratton, Richard. "The Rolling Stone Interview Part I: Aquarius Hustling." *Rolling Stone*, January 2, 1975, pp. 40ff; Part II, *Rolling Stone*, January 16. 1975. pp. 42ff.

Tanner, Tony. *City of Words: American Fiction 1950-1970.* New York: Harper & Row, 1971.

Thorp, Willard. *American Writing in the Twentieth Century.* Cambridge: Harvard University Press, 1960.

Toback, James. "At Play in the Fields of the Bored." *Esquire*, December 1968, p. 150.

Wagenheim, Allan J. "Square's Progress: *An American Dream*." *Critique* 10:45-68.

Weales, Gerald. *The Jumping-Off Place: American Drama in the 1960's.* New York: Macmillan, 1969.

Weber, Brom. "A Fear of Dying: Norman Mailer's *An American Dream*," *Hollins Critic* 2 (June 1965): 1-6, 8-11.

Whitman, Walt. "Democratic Vistas," In *The Collected Works of Walt Whitman: Prose Works, 1892*, edited by Floyd Stovall. Vol. 2. New York: New York University Press, 1964.

INDEX

Index

Index

Marx, Karl, 13, 19, 46, 58, 59, 87
Marx, Leo, 5, 83
McCarthy, Eugene, 155, 174
McGovern, George, 171, 172, 173, 174
McLuhan, Marshall, 108, 109, 111
Melville, Herman, 23-24, 40, 46, 119, 161
Mencken, H. L., 162
Miami and the Siege of Chicago, 137n, 149, 152-58, 163, 171
Miller, Arthur, 175
Miller, Henry, 9, 55, 96, 102, 165
Millett, Kate, 165, 166, 167
Milton, John, 60
Moby Dick, 24, 158
Monroe, Marilyn, 96, 103, 174-78
Morales, Adele, 56, 67
Morris, Willie, 163
Mudrick, Marvin, 27
Muste, John M., 65n
Naked and the Dead, The, 6, 10, 15, 16, 24, 28, 29, 30, 34, 35, 37, 38, 39, 43, 116, 122
Naked Lunch, 14, 100, 114
Nixon, Richard, 153-54, 172, 173
Norman Mailer: A Comprehensive Bibliography, 65n
Oates, Joyce Carol, 14
O'Brien, Lawrence, 174
Of a Fire on the Moon, 16, 17, 96, 137n, 141, 154, 158-63, 166-67, 174, 176
Orwell, George, 87
Paradise Lost, 92
Patterson, Floyd, 170
Piers Plowman, 42
Plimpton, George, 142
Podhoretz, Norman, 60, 122
Poe, Edgar Allen, 89, 119
Poirier, Richard, 8, 9, 19, 150
Polsky, Ned, 58
Presidential Papers, The, 16, 21, 31, 67, 69, 71-72, 73, 74, 81, 105, 121, 143, 169, 170
Prisoner of Sex, The, 137n, 149, 163-67, 168
Proust, Marcel, 13
Red Badge of Courage, The, 37

Reich, Charles, 135
Reich, Wilhelm, 55, 57
Reisman, David, 46
Remembrance of Things Past, 180
Rideout, Walter B., 65n
Ring and the Book, The, 52
Rosoff, Peter, 143
Roth, Philip, 60
Running Against the Machine, 139
St. George and the Godfather, 137n, 149, 150, 171-74
Salinger, J. D., 18
Samuels, Charles T., 137n
Sartre, Jean Paul, 84, 122
Scarlet Letter, The, 41
Schulz, Max F., 65n
Sexual Politics, 165-66
Shaw, George Bernard, 57
Shelley, Percy Bysshe, 65n
Sound and the Fury, The, 18, 37
Spengler, Oswald, 13
Stalin, Joseph, 40, 42
Stark, John Olsen, 40, 108, 149, 155
Steffins, Lincoln, 136
Steinbeck, John, 11, 12, 15, 24
Stendhal, 13, 69
Stern, Richard G., 58
Stratton, Rick, 175
Styron, William, 14, 64n
Tanner, Tony, 9, 98n, 137n
Thoreau, Henry David, 136
Thorp, Willard, 65n
Toback, James, 180n
Tolstoy, Leo, 13, 20, 69, 179
Torn, Rip, 142, 145, 146, 147
Torres, José, 142, 146, 150
Twain, Mark, 23, 79
U.S.A., 37
Updike, John, 60
Vidal, Gore, 150
Voltaire, François, 138, 171
Vonnegut, Kurt, 14
Wagenheim, Allan J., 88
Walden, 136
Wallace, George, 151
Wallace, Henry, 46
Wallace, Mike, 175
War and Peace, 180

191

Index